MY FIRST GOLDEN
ENCYCLOPEDIA

CONSULTANT   BERTHA MORRIS PARKER

BY JANE WERNER WATSON

PICTURES BY WILLIAM DUGAN

GOLDEN PRESS • NEW YORK
Western Publishing Company, Inc.

FOREWORD

No stage of a child's education is as important as the beginning. The three-year-old child, able to walk and therefore to explore, able to talk and therefore to ask questions, is a living bundle of curiosity about everything around him. For the next few years, the period just before and after starting school and learning to read, it is literally impossible for a child to learn too much. At this stage, learning is as natural as breathing. Later on come the more formal aspects of education, exercises and tests, assignments and homework, but from three to eight learning is life itself. MY FIRST GOLDEN ENCYCLOPEDIA, with more than 350 pages of text and 1,500 illustrations, has been meticulously planned both to arouse and satisfy the thirst for knowledge of this age group.

When *The Golden Book Encyclopedia* was first presented to the public, the publishers were gratified to receive an unusually large number of letters from parents telling how much their children liked it. An interesting sidelight of many of these letters was that, despite the fact that *The Golden Book Encyclopedia* was designed for children from eight to twelve, many parents found that their younger children, even those who could not read, found it just as fascinating as the older ones. Some parents even bought two sets. Why, they asked, could not a similar group of books be planned especially for these younger children? MY FIRST GOLDEN ENCYCLOPEDIA, after years of planning, is the result of this interest.

Jane Werner Watson, the author of over a hundred Golden Books, including the best-selling *Golden History of the World* and *The New Golden Encyclopedia*, was asked to prepare the text. A writer with the rare ability to communicate successfully with the very young, Mrs. Watson has managed to present a great deal of basically complex information in a way that will fascinate children as much as their favorite bedtime story.

The chief consultant for the ENCYCLOPEDIA has been Dr. Bertha Morris Parker, herself a pioneer in writing non-fiction for very young children and author of the famous *Golden Book Encyclopedia*. Dr. Parker has checked every word of the text to insure that it is readable, interesting, informative and accurate. The full-color illustrations by William Dugan were carefully executed to reflect and augment the information given in the text. They are also, we think you will agree, delightful in themselves.

MY FIRST GOLDEN ENCYCLOPEDIA has been printed and bound with the distinction expected of all Golden Books. Our best hope for this volume is that over the years it will become dog-eared and thoroughly tattered. That is the surest sign of a truly successful children's book. —THE PUBLISHERS

1971 Edition

GOLDEN, GOLDEN BOOK, and GOLDEN PRESS® are trademarks of Western Publishing Company, Inc.
Library of Congress Catalog Card Number: 69-20440

abacus

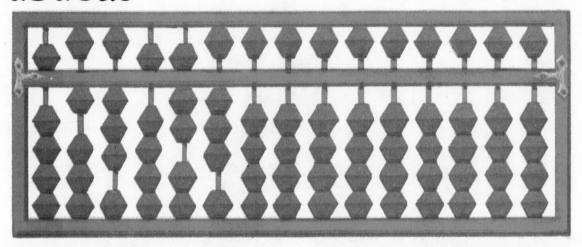

An abacus has beads on wires.
Some beads stand for 1.
Some beads stand for 10.
Some beads stand
    for other numbers.
People in many lands count
    and do arithmetic
    on an abacus.

They move the beads
    on the wires.
They add.
They subtract.
They do many things
    with numbers
    by moving the beads
    on the abacus.

accordion

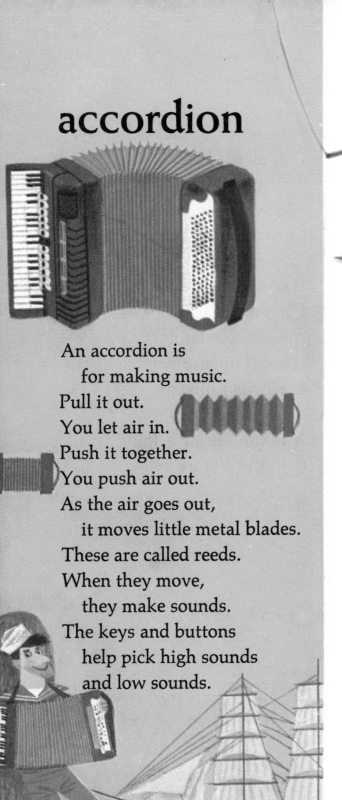

An accordion is
  for making music.
Pull it out.
You let air in.
Push it together.
You push air out.
As the air goes out,
  it moves little metal blades.
These are called reeds.
When they move,
  they make sounds.
The keys and buttons
  help pick high sounds
  and low sounds.

acrobat

An acrobat is strong and nimble.
He can do many tricks
  with his body.
He must exercise.
He must eat well.
He must practice each trick
  many times.
Thus he learns to do it well.

air

Air is all around us.
We breathe it all the time.
We do not see air.
But we feel it move.

Sometimes air moves lightly.
We call it a breeze.
Sometimes air moves fast.
We call it a wind.
Moving air gives us
    our weather.
(Look up *weather* and *wind*.)
Sometimes air helps us.
It turns windmills.
It holds up airplanes.
It pushes sailboats
    over the water.
You can see air helping
    in the picture below.

aircraft

Airplanes fly in the air.
Many airplanes
 have propellers.
The motors turn
 the propellers.
The propellers turn very fast.
They turn so fast
 that it is hard to see
 their curved blades.
The propeller blades bite
 into the air ahead.

They pull the airplane forward.
Airplanes have wings.
Air pushes down on the wings
 from above.
Air pushes up on the wings
 from below.
The shape of the wings
 makes the air push up
 more than down.
The air holds
 the airplane up.

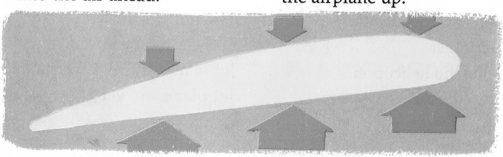

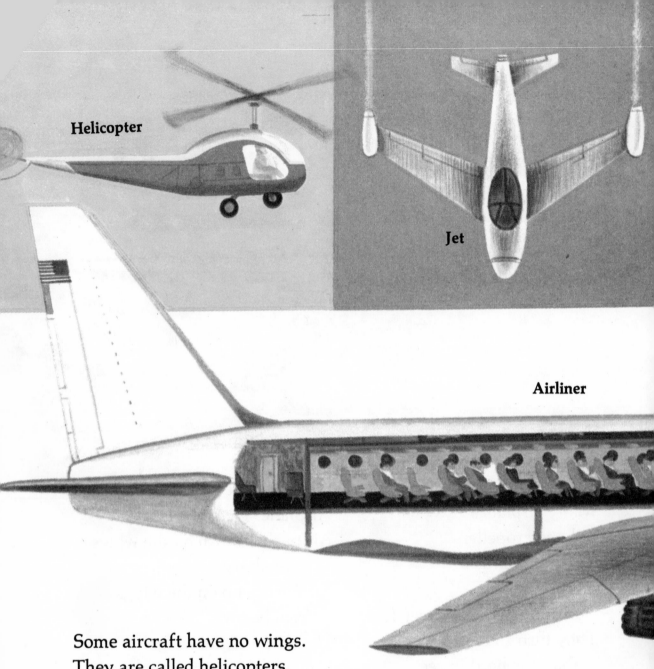

Helicopter

Jet

Airliner

Some aircraft have no wings.
They are called helicopters.
A helicopter has
   a very large propeller on top.
This is called a rotor.
The rotor goes around
   very fast.
It pulls the helicopter
   into the air.

Some planes have jet engines.
Hot gas pours out of the jets.
The hot gas pushes
   the airplane ahead.
Jet planes fly very, very fast.
Jet planes fly very, very high.

The man who flies an airplane
   is called a pilot.
The pilot sits up in front
   in the cockpit.
A big airplane needs
   a man to check
   on its direction.
This man is the navigator.
He sits in the cockpit too.

There is a radio man.
He talks to people on the ground.
They tell him about the weather.
They tell him when the pilot
   can land the plane.
The radio man sits
   in the cockpit too.
All these men are members
   of the crew of a big airplane.

Cockpit

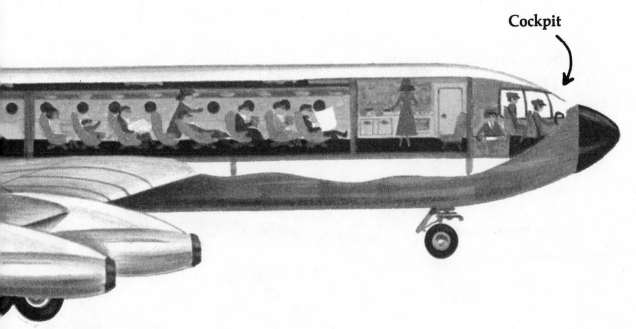

The passengers
   in an airplane sit in the cabin.
They may read or write
   or sleep or talk
   or eat meals from trays.
Or they may look out of
   the windows.

Stewards or hostesses
   make the passengers comfortable
   and serve them meals.
Their kitchen is very small.
   It is called a galley.

Some airplanes are small.
They hold one or two people.

Some small airplanes spray fields
to kill insects.
They are called crop dusters.

Some airplanes are big.
They may hold more than
a hundred people.

Some airplanes look
for forest fires.

Some airplanes carry cameras
to take pictures.

Some helicopters carry mail
into town from the airport.

Helicopters can land
in a very small space.
Or they can come down low
to drop ropes to people
who need help.

Seaplanes have pontoons
like small boats
instead of wheels.
They land on water.

Some planes can land either
on water or on the ground.
They are called amphibians.

airport

Airplanes land at airports.
An airport has runways.
Runways are roads
 for airplanes
 when they are
 on the ground.

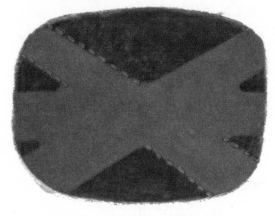

At night, colored lights
 show where the runways are.

An airport has a **control tower**.
Men in the control tower
 talk to the crew
 in planes by radio.
(Look up *radio*.)
The men in the control tower
 tell the plane crew
 when and where to land
 and take off.

An airport has hangars.
Airplanes are parked
    in hangars.
Mechanics keep the planes
    in good shape for flying.

An airport has a terminal.
People who want to travel
    in an airplane
    wait for it
    in the terminal.

13

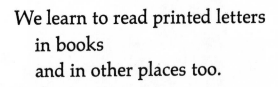

alphabet

Our alphabet is made up
   of 26 letters.
The letters stand for sounds.
We put letters together
   to write words.

We learn to read printed letters
   in books
and in other places too.

The letters on the blocks
   are small letters.
We use small letters most.
All the small letters
   are at the top of the page.
The letters on the sign below
   are capital letters.
We use them
   at the beginning of names.
We use them at the beginning
   of sentences.

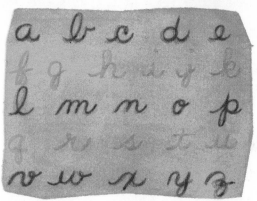

When you write a word
   you use letters like this.

hen

or like this

n o p q r s t u v w x y z

Greece

Israel

Saudi Arabia

In some other lands
people use other letters
to make words.
They have other alphabets.

animals

Some living things are plants.
All the others are animals.
There are twenty-three
   animals in these pictures.
Most animals can move about.
Most plants cannot.

Some animals are very,
   very small.
We need a magnifying glass
   to see them.
Many of the tiniest animals
   live in water.

Two-Spotted   Striped
Ladybird   Cucumber Beetle

Luna Moth

More than half of all
   the kinds of animals
   are insects.

There are seven insects
   in these pictures.
The two caterpillars
   are baby insects.
The other insects
   are grown-up.
Grown-up insects
   have six legs.
Most grown-up insects
   have wings and can fly

Toucan

Rhinoceros

Hippopotamus

Alligator   **Turtle**

Frog

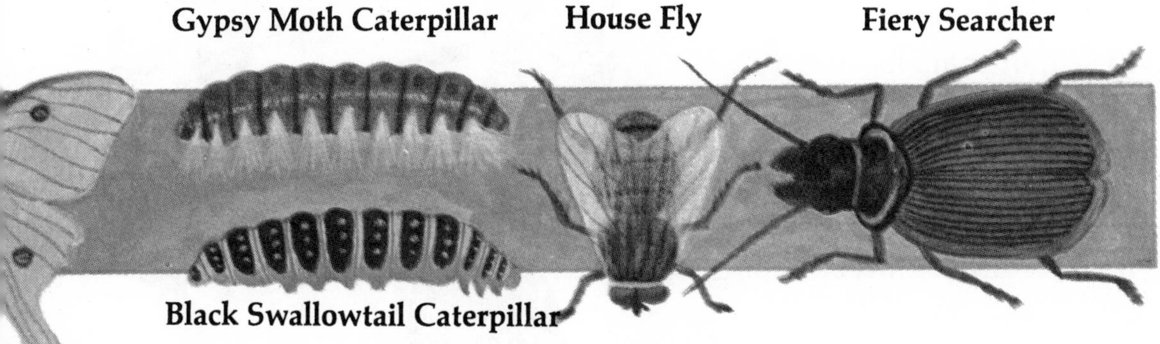

Gypsy Moth Caterpillar **House Fly** **Fiery Searcher**

Black Swallowtail Caterpillar

Five of these animals
    are birds.
All birds have feathers.
The turtle and the alligator
    are reptiles.
Reptiles are covered
    with scales.

The frog is an amphibian.
Amphibians live
    partly on land,
    partly in the water.
The rabbit and the squirrel
    are mammals.
So are the five biggest
    animals in the picture.

Camel

Bluebird

Meadowlark

Elephant

Ostrich

**Crowned
Crane**

Lion

Squirrel

Rabbit

17

Here are eight
  more mammals.
Most mammals have
  coats of fur.
All mammals have
  some hair.
Most mammals have
  four legs.
Mammal mothers feed
  their babies milk
  until the babies
  are old enough
  to eat other food.
Dogs are mammals.
Cats are mammals.
Cows and horses and pigs
  are mammals.
People are mammals, too.
Whales are the
  biggest mammals.
Shrews are the littlest.
Reptiles and amphibians
  have bones.
So do birds and mammals.

Tiger

Monkey

Shrew

Bear

Giraffe

Donkey

Raccoon

Okapi

Fishes have bones, too.
All fishes live in water.
Crabs and clams and
    many other water animals
    have shells instead of bones.
The red animal is a squid.
(You will find more
    about many animals
    on other pages.
Look for them.)

aquarium

An aquarium is a glass home
    for fish and other
    water animals or plants.

Arctic

It is cold in the Arctic.
There are no trees.
There are few animals.
There are very few people.
The plants are small.
But there is lots
    of ice and snow.

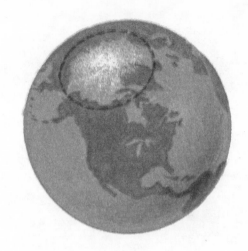

The North Pole is in the Arctic.
There are even colder lands
    around the South Pole.
We call them the Antarctic.

art

Making something beautiful
  is an art.
You may make something
  beautiful of clay
  or with finger paints
  or with crayons.
You may do a beautiful dance.
You may sing a song beautifully.
All of these are works of art.
When you make something
  beautiful, you are an artist.

automobile

An automobile, or car,
must have an engine.

Hood

Most engines are under
the hood in front.
Some are at the back
of the car.
Most automobile engines
need gasoline.
The engine makes the wheels
turn.
The turning wheels
make the car run,
so we can go for a ride.

The first automobiles were
called "horseless carriages."
The automobile did not need
horses to move it.
It moved by itself.
Automobile means
"self-moving."

The automobile has a frame
called a chassis.
We say "chass-ee."
The automobile has a body
which fits on the chassis.
The body has doors
and windows.
It has seats inside.
It has space for luggage.

The engine fits on the chassis.
The hood covers the engine.
The steering wheel's post
leads to the front wheels.
It turns the wheels to the right
or to the left.
Many automobiles have heaters
and radios to make trips
more pleasant.

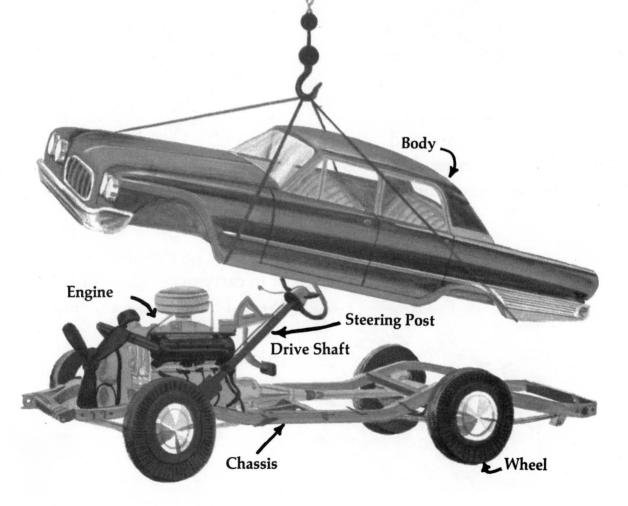

Body

Engine

Steering Post

Drive Shaft

Chassis

Wheel

23

Many families
  have automobiles
  called station wagons.
These have lots of room
  for children and groceries
  and other things.

Very small cars are good
  for short trips.
Their engines do not use
  much gasoline.

Where roads are bad
  special cars are used.
Some of them are called jeeps.
They are very strong.

There are special cars
  to carry many kinds of loads.
We call them trucks and buses.
(Look up *bus*.)
(Also, look up *travel*
  and *transportation*.)

ball

A ball is round.
This seal is playing
   with a ball.
We play games
   with balls, too.
We play baseball.
We play basketball.
We play many ball games.

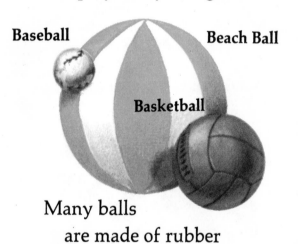

Baseball   **Beach Ball**

Basketball

Many balls
   are made of rubber
   so they bounce.

Our world is shaped like a ball.

balloon

A balloon
   is a kind of ball.
Some balloons
   are lighter than air.
They have a light gas inside.
They float in the air.

Weather Balloon

Some balloons can
   float high in the sky.
Men send these big balloons up
   to find out what the weather
   is like high in the sky.
They are called weather balloons.

Passenger Balloon

Before the days of airplanes
men who wanted to fly
rode in baskets
tied to very large balloons.

Army Blimp

Some balloons
even had engines.
These were called airships
or dirigibles.

banana

A banana is a fruit.
Bananas grow in bunches.
A banana plant has
just one bunch of bananas.
Bananas grow where it is hot.
There people eat bananas
almost every day.
Sometimes they fry them
or bake them
or mash them.

band

A band plays loud
and lively music.
The bandsmen march
in parades.
They have drums
and horns
and big trombones.

bank

We save money in a bank.

A big bank keeps a record
of money we put in
or take out of the bank.
A bank loans money to people
to buy such things as
houses or cars.
People pay back the money.
And they pay the bank
for letting them use it.

bark

Bark protects
the trunk
and branches
of a tree.
A tree cannot live
if all its bark is taken off.
(Look up *trees* and *cork*.)

basket

Baskets are **made**
in many sizes
and shapes
to hold
many kinds of things.

A basket is **woven**.
The strips **go in and out**.
Many baskets are woven
of reeds.
The reeds **bend best**
when they are fresh
or damp.

bear

Bears are big furry animals.
Bears can stand up
  on their back legs.
Some stand taller
  than a man.
Bears eat many sweet things.
They eat honey made by bees.
They eat ripe sweet berries.
Bears eat bugs and fish
  and wild onions too.
They eat and grow fat.
In winter they sleep.
They live on their fat.
Baby bear cubs
  are born during late winter.
Polar bears live in the north.
Their fur is almost as white
  as the ice and snow.

There are black bears
  and brown bears
  and yellow-red bears.
There are many kinds of bears.
Most of them can climb trees.

beaver

The beaver is an animal
    that builds.
Beavers nibble trees
    with their strong teeth
    until the trees fall down.
They chew off branches.
They drag them to a stream.
They build a dam
    across the stream.
The dam is made of branches
    packed with mud.

The beaver packs the mud hard
    with its flat tail.
Slap, slap, slap, goes the tail.
The dam holds back the water.
The water forms a pond.
In the pond
    the beaver builds its house
    of branches and mud.
Most of the house is hidden
    under water.
The beaver raises its family there.
(Look up *dam*.)

bee

A bee is an insect.
(Look up *insects*.)
This bee is a honeybee.
Honeybees live together.
Some people set up hives
for bee swarms to live in.

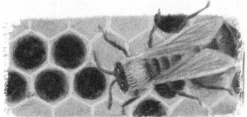

Bee in Honeycomb

In every hive
there is a queen.
She lays eggs.
There are many worker bees.
They build honeycombs.
They guard the hive.
The worker bees collect nectar
from flowers.
The bee rests on a flower.
It laps up nectar
with its tongue.
It sucks the nectar
into its honey sac.
Then the bee takes the nectar
back to the honeycomb.

The nectar turns into honey
in the honeycomb.
When the hive is full of honey,
the beekeeper puts on
a special hood and gloves
and takes out the honey.
He needs the hood and gloves
so that bees guarding the hive
will not sting him.
A bee sting hurts.
But it is hard on the bee too.
When it leaves its stinger
in a person, the bee dies.

Unicorn Beetle

beetle

A beetle is an insect.
It has two pairs of wings.
The outer wings are hard.
They cover the inner wings.
The beetle uses the thin
inner wings to fly.
There are many, many kinds
of beetles.
Here are a few of them.

Locust Borer

Carrion Beetle

Striped Blister Beetle

bells

Bells ring.
They go ding dong ding
  or BONG BONG
  or cling clang cling.

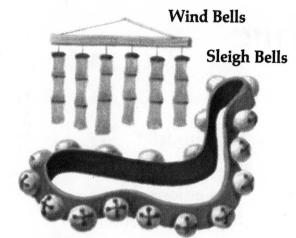

Wind Bells

Sleigh Bells

Cow Bell

Bells call us to school
  and to church.

Church Bells in Belfry

Some bells sound sweet.
Some bells sound loud.
Some bells sound sweetly sad.

Most bells are made of metal.
Inside the bell
  is a piece of metal.
It is called a clapper.
When the bell swings,
  the clapper strikes the side,
  and the bell rings.
Some bells are struck
  with hammers instead.

berries

Berries have seeds in them.
Some berries are sour.
Some are sweet.
Some are not good to eat.

bicycle

A bicycle has two wheels.
You pedal with your feet
  to make it go.
The first bicycles
  had no foot pedals.

Early Bicycle

The rider had to push
  his feet against the ground.
Some old-time bicycles
  had one big wheel
  and one small one.
Some bicycles have two seats.
They are called tandems.
Bi-means two
Uni-means one.
A unicycle has only
  one wheel.

It is hard
  to keep your balance
  on a unicycle.
Not many people ride them.
But a bicycle is easy to ride.
Tri-means three.
A tricycle has three wheels.
Many children ride tricycles.
Motorcycles are heavy bicycles
  with motors.
Some have a side car
  for an extra passenger.

Early Bicycle

Tricycle

Unicycle

bird

Sandpiper

Birds are the only
  animals
  with feathers.
A bird has two legs
  and two wings.

Owl

Most birds can fly.
They have hollow bones
  with air inside.
The hollow shafts
  of their feathers
  have air inside.
Most birds are very light.
They spread their strong wings
  and the air holds them up.
Their hearts beat very fast,
  like tiny engines.
They can move their wings
  very fast.
And they fly.

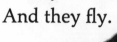

Toucan

Hummingbird

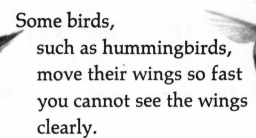

Some birds,
  such as hummingbirds,
  move their wings so fast
  you cannot see the wings
  clearly.
Penguins are birds that
  cannot fly
  because their wings
  are too small.

**Penguin
with baby**

They live in lands
  of ice and snow
  near the South Pole.
Ostriches are the
  biggest birds of all.

Ostrich

Their wings are too small
  to lift their heavy bodies.
They cannot fly.
But they can run very fast
  across the desert.

Most birds
    build nests.
They build
    in trees
    or in bushes
    or on the ground.

Birds lay eggs in their nests.

Cardinal

They stay on the nests
    to keep the eggs warm.

Baby birds hatch
    from the eggs.
The mother and father birds
    bring their babies food.
Soon the young birds
    are strong enough
    to leave the nest.

Some birds can fly
    hundreds of miles
    over land and sea.
Many birds of the north
    fly to the warm south
    for the winter.

They fly north when summer
    comes.
Some birds always live
    near water.
Some live near ponds.
Some live near swamps.
Some live near the shores
    of lakes or seas.

blood

If you prick your finger,
   blood comes out.
The blood in our bodies
   is important.
Blood carries food we eat
   and air we breathe
   through our bodies
   to where they are needed.
Our hearts pump
   day and night
   to keep the blood moving.
It moves away from the heart
   through arteries
   and back to the heart
   through the veins.

boat

Boats float.
They float on water.
We can ride in a boat
   on the water and stay dry.

Most boats are made of wood.

Some boats are made of skins

or of metal

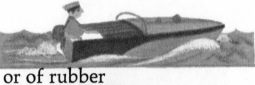

or of rubber

or of reeds

or of the bark of trees.

They move with paddles
   or oars or motors
   or are pushed along
   by the wind.

body

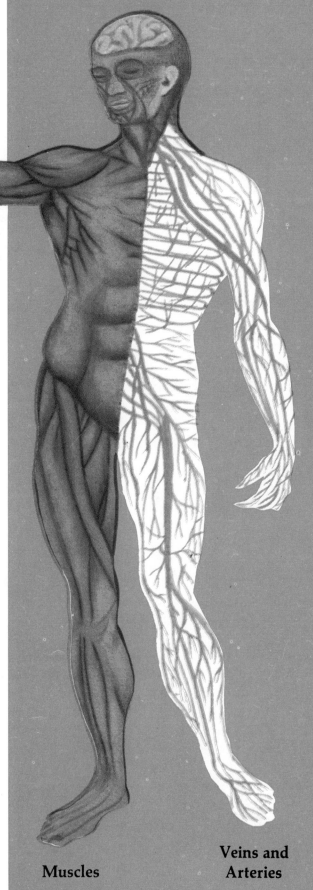

Your body has a head,
    a trunk, two arms, and two legs.
You have hands.
You have fingers and thumbs.
Some other animals have
    paws like hands.
But few animals
    have thumbs like yours.
You have feet.
You have eyes and ears
    and a nose to tell you
    about the world around you.
You have nerves
    to carry messages
    and muscles
    to move your bones.
You have a brain
    inside your head.
Nerves and muscles and brain
    make your eyes and ears
    and nose
    and your hands and feet
    work together to do
    what you want to do.

Muscles

Veins and
Arteries

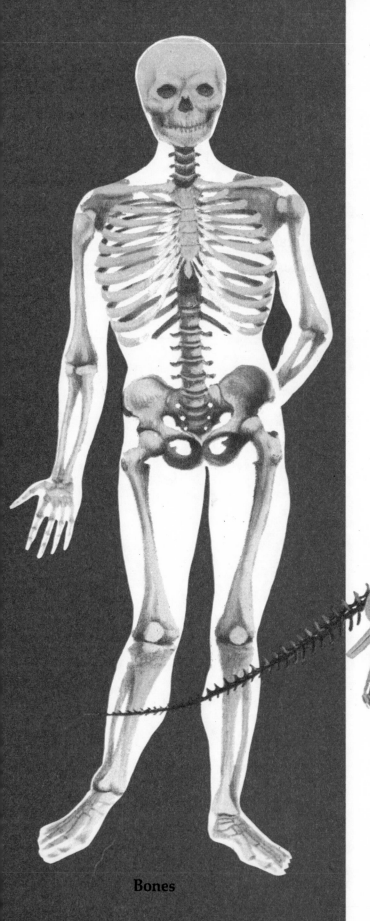

Bones

bone

Bones inside your body
give your body strength
and shape.
Without bones you could not
stand or sit or walk.
You would not be a person
without bones.
You have about 200 bones.
Over your bones you have
muscle and a little fat
and a smooth covering of skin.
Bones are put together
at joints.
Most large animals have bones.

**Diplodocus
skeleton**

The picture shows the bones
of a large prehistoric animal.
A whole set of bones
is called a skeleton.
(Look up *skeleton*.)

book

A book may tell a story.
It may have pictures.
It may teach something.
In olden days books
    were written by hand.

Pictures were
    painted by hand
    in those books.

Some were very beautiful.
Some books in olden days
    did not have pages.

The book was one long strip,
    or scroll,
        rolled up at both ends.
As you read
    you rolled up one side.
You unrolled the other side.
These old books
    were not written on **paper**.

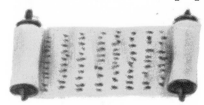

They were written
    on parchment
    made from animal skins,
    or on papyrus
    made from reeds.

Horn books had their pages
    covered with thin sheets
    of horn.
No one owned many books
    in olden days.
Now books are printed
    by machine
    on paper.
We can have lots of them.

bread

Bread is to eat.
Bread is made from flour
   and water or milk.
Most flour is made from grain.
The grain is ground up fine.
The grain in flour
   may be wheat or rye
   or corn or oats.
We can have wheat bread
   or rye bread
   or corn bread
   or oatmeal bread
   or even other kinds.

Most bread is shaped
   into loaves or rolls.
It is baked in an oven.
A loaf of bread
   may be flat and heavy
   or high and light.
But all kinds of bread
   are good to eat.

brick

Oven-baked bricks
   are very hard.
They last a long, long time.
Many buildings
   are made of baked bricks.

Bricks are for building.
Most bricks are made of clay.
Some bricks are baked
   in ovens called kilns.
Some bricks are dried
   in the sun.

Fireplaces
   are often made of bricks.
For the insides of fireplaces
   special fire brick is used.

These bricks are simple to make.

Some clay bricks are hollow.
They are called tile.

Some bricks are made
   of glass.

They do not cost much.
But they are not very hard.
Sun-dried bricks
   may melt in rain.
The house made of them
   may fall.

A wall of glass bricks
   lets light come through.
But still the wall is very
   strong.

bridge

A bridge crosses a river
   or a highway
   or railroad tracks.
We can walk or ride safely
   over water or
   over traffic
   on a bridge.

Most bridges today are made
   of steel.
Steel is very strong
   even in thin strips.
The bridge can be strong and
   still look light and graceful.

Many old bridges
   are made of stone.
They are very strong and heavy.

Some old bridges are
   made of wood

or of rope.

Some bridges float in water.

buffalo

There are water buffalo
  in many lands.
They are hard-working animals.
They give milk.
They draw plows.
They are called water buffalo
  because they can work
  in water.

This animal is often called
  a buffalo.
Its real name
  is the American bison.
Bison used to wander
  in great herds
  over the western plains.

bug

Shield Bug

Bugs are insects.
They can stick their beaks
  into animals or plants
  and suck out their juices.
Their outer wings are so thin
  you can see through them.

Large Milkweed Bug

Tarnished Plant Bug

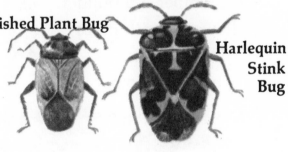

**Harlequin
Stink
Bug**

All bugs are insects.
But not all insects are bugs.
(Look up *insects*.)

builders

Many kinds of builders
    work on a building.
A carpenter is a builder.
He works with wood.
A mason is a builder.
He works with stone
    or bricks.
He puts them together
    with mortar.
A plumber is a builder.
He works with pipes
    for kitchens
    and bathrooms.

An electrician
    is a builder.
He works with wiring
    for lights
    and stoves.

buildings

Buildings shelter us from wind
    and rain,
    from cold and
    from the sun's heat.
We live in houses
    or apartments.

These are buildings.
We go to school in buildings
    called schools.

Some people work
    in buildings called factories.

Some people work
in office buildings.
In big cities
office buildings
may be very tall.
Tall buildings
are called
skyscrapers.
Their tops do seem to scrape
the sky.

When we are sick
we go to buildings
called hospitals.

We worship in buildings
called churches or temples.

Men have built themselves
shelters for thousands of years.
They learned to use
what was handy,
and they still do.

Where there was stone
they built stone buildings.

Where there were trees
they built wood buildings.
Sometimes they used round logs.

More often they sawed the logs
into flat planks.
Where there was clay
they made bricks.

Some men made houses
    of reeds
    plastered with mud.
Some built with chunks
    of sod cut out of the ground.

Some built with chunks
    of icy snow.

Today buildings are made
    of wood and brick,
    of stone and steel,
    of concrete and glass,
    of reeds and grass,
    of sod and snow,
    and even of paper.

bus

A bus carries people
    to school
    or to work
    or to a shop
    or from one city to another.
It stops for people
    who wait for it at a bus stop.
On most buses the people
    pay a fare.
The bus driver collects
    the money
    the people pay.

butterflies and moths

Gypsy Moth

Alfalfa Butterfly

Butterflies and moths
  are insects.
Like most insects
  they are "turn-into"
  animals.
Grown-up butterflies
  and moths lay eggs.
The eggs hatch
  into caterpillars.
Some caterpillars
  eat plant leaves.
Some eat fruits and vegetables.

Morning Cloak Larva

The caterpillars of some moths
  eat wool clothes.
Some spin cocoons
  or form chrysalises
  to sleep in.

When the caterpillars
  are fully grown
  they go to sleep.
These resting insects
  are called pupae.
When they wake up
  they come out of their cocoons
  or chrysalises.
They sit in the sun
  while their new wings dry.
Then they fly away.
They are pretty butterflies
  or moths.

Morning Cloak Chrysalis

Morning Cloak Butterfly

Most butterflies fly about
  in the daytime.

Most moths fly
　　at night.
Grown-up moths and butterflies
　　do not eat much.
They do not live long.
But they lay eggs
　　which turn into caterpillars
　　which turn into pupae
　　which turn into
　　grown-up moths
　　and butterflies.
(Look up *insects*.)

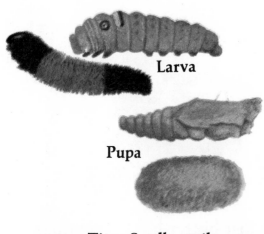

Larva

Pupa

**Tiger Swallowtail
Butterfly**

Isabella Moth

buttons and buttonholes

Buttons and buttonholes
　　help hold our clothes together.
Buttons look nice too.
Some are very pretty.

They are used for decoration.

Sometimes we use
　　hooks and eyes
　　instead of buttons.
Sometimes we use snaps.

Sometimes we use zippers.

Sometimes we use pins.
But buttons look nicest.

cactus

Cactus plants grow
in the desert.
It is very dry there.
(Look up *desert*.)
Cactus plants
have thick stems.
They store water
in their stems.
Instead of leaves
they have spines
called needles.
The needles help keep them safe
from hungry animals.

camel

Camels live in the desert.
They store fat in their humps.
Some camels have one hump.
Some have two humps.
They have padded feet
and special eyelashes
to protect them from the sand.
They can travel far
across the desert.

A caravan is a train of camels.

calendar

A calendar shows the days
of the week—
Sunday, Monday, Tuesday,
Wednesday, Thursday,
Friday, Saturday.
A calendar shows the months
of the year—
January, February, March,
April, May, June, July,
August, September, October,
November, December.
It shows the days of the month.
"Thirty days hath September,
April, June and November.
All the rest have thirty-one
Save February which alone
has twenty-eight."
A calendar shows holidays
like Christmas.
It has your birthday on it, too.

camera

A camera takes pictures.
It has a little hole in front
    to let light in for a moment
    when you click the shutter.
The light makes a pattern
    on the film inside.
The pattern on the film
    can be printed
    on special paper.
Then you have a picture.
Some cameras take
    many pictures very fast.
We call them motion picture
    cameras.
We see those pictures
    on a big screen
    instead of on paper.

camp

We camp out-of-doors.
In many camps
    people sleep in tents.

They spend their days
    outside.
They play games
    and swim.
They learn to make things
    with their hands.
Camping is fun.

canal

A canal is a waterway
    cut by men.
A canal may lead water
    to dry fields.
A canal may connect
    two lakes or two rivers,
    two seas or two oceans,
    or other bodies of water.
If one lake or ocean
    is higher than the other,
    the canal has locks.
A boat floats into a lock.
Gates are closed at both ends.
Water is let in or out
    until the boat
    is at the right level
    to float out
    into the other ocean or lake.

candle

A candle gives light as it burns.
A candle has a string
    down its middle.
The string is called a wick.
Around the wick is wax.
The wick keeps the wax
    burning evenly.
In olden days people used candles
    to light their homes.

They made their own candles.
Sometimes they dipped
   a row of wicks
   into hot wax or fat
   until enough stuck
   to make a candle.
Sometimes they strung the wicks
   down through molds
   and poured in wax
   to fill the molds.
A large room could be lighted
   with hundreds of candles
   hung in a chandelier.
Sometimes people stood
   candles in bases
   called candelabra.
Sometimes they used
   a single candle
   in a candlestick just as we do.
Candles are fun
   on a birthday cake.

candy

Candy is sweet.
Most candy is made
   with sugar.
Some is made with honey.
The sugar or honey
   may hold together
   nuts or dates or figs.
Often candy has chocolate in it.
Or it is dipped in chocolate.

card

A card is a piece of stiff paper.
A set of cards with pictures
   can be used for playing games.
A set of playing cards
   is called a deck.
Or a card may have a message.
We may send a post card
   or greeting card
   through the mail.

castle

In olden times kings and queens
  and knights and ladies
  often lived in castles.
Castles were built of stone.
They had strong gates.
They had high walls.
Soldiers watched on the walls.
Often a ditch called a moat
  was dug around the castle.
The moat was filled with water.
If enemies came,
  the people from the villages
  near the castle
  hurried inside the walls.
There was room for many people
  inside the castle walls.

Then soldiers raised the drawbridg
  over the moat.
So it was hard for an enemy
  to get into the castle.
There was room for soldiers
  and horses and supplies of food.
There were big rooms
  where people lived.
But the rooms were cold and bare.
A castle was not a cheery place
  to live.

cat

Siamese

Persian

Tabby

A cat moves quietly.
It has soft pads on its feet.
A cat eats meat.
It hunts for its food.
It hunts mostly at night.
It can see well at night.
It has sharp claws and teeth.
The cats we know best
   live with people.

The animals below
   are wild animals.
They are members
   of the cat family,
   too.

Cheetah

Tiger

Lion

cattle and cows

We owe many things to cattle.
We eat their meat.
We call it beef.
Cows are cattle.
From their milk we get cream
    and butter,
    cheese and ice cream.

From their skins we get
    leather to make
    handbags and suitcases,
    belts and shoes
    and warm leather jackets.
And if there were no cattle
    there would be no cowboys
    in the West
    to watch the herds of cattle
    as they feed on the range!

caves and cavemen

A cave is a hollow
    in a wall of rock.
Some caves are as big
    as rooms, or bigger.
Some animals live in caves.
Bears often spend
    the winter in caves.
Long, long years ago
    people lived in caves.
We call them cave men.
In the caves we find stone tools
    they used.

We find bones
    of animals they ate.
We find drawings
    they made on the walls.
That is how we know
    there were cave men.

cheese

Cheese is good to eat.
It is made in many lands.
It has many shapes and tastes.
Cheese is good for us.
Cheese is made from milk.

The milk stands.
It separates.
Part is thick.
We call the thick part curds.
Part is thin and watery.
We call this part whey.
Cheese is made from the curds.

circle

A circle is round.
Every place on its edge
  is the same distance
  from its center.
All wheels are circles.
(Look up *wheel*.)
This clock face is a circle.
We make a circle
  to play some games.

circus

A circus is a show
  in a ring.
A ring is round.
It is a circle.
A circus has acrobats.
(Look up *acrobat*.)

C

Acrobats swing high in the air.
They walk on high wires.
A circus has trained animals.
And a circus has funny clowns.
A circus travels
    from town to town.

In a tent or hall
    it sets up its ring and seats.
Then the band plays.
Crowds of people come.
And the show in the ring begins.
Seeing a circus is fun!

city

A city has many buildings.
A city has many people.
A city is a busy, crowded place.
Many cities are built
  on rivers or lakes or seas.

Ships and boats
  and trains and planes
  bring loads of goods
  to be sold in city stores.
A city has many streets.
Cars and trucks, buses and taxis
  fill the streets.
A city is a busy place.
A city has many stores.

The stores sell food and clothing
   and all sorts of things.
A city has factories.
Things are made in the factories
   to be sold in stores.
(Look up *factory*.)
A city has many homes.
Some are big
   apartment buildings.
They hold many families.

Some are one-family houses.
(Look up *house*.)
A city has schools and churches.
It has parks to play in.
It has policemen to keep order.
It has firemen to put out fires.
A city has so many people
   doing so many
   different things!
A city is a busy, busy place.

cliff dwellers and dwellings

Long ago some Indians
  built houses in cliffs.
They built whole cities there.
It was hard for enemies
  to climb steep cliffs
  to harm them.
So the people felt safe.
They raised their crops
  down in the valley.
At night they climbed
  up to their cliff homes.
We call these people
  cliff dwellers.

clock

winding stem

minute hand

hour hand

second hand

A clock tells the time.
A clock face has numbers
  for the hours.
1,2,3,4,5,6,7,
8,9,10,11,12.
A clock face has hands.
It has a short hand
  to point to the hours.
It has a long hand
  to point to the minutes.

Inside most clocks
   are wheels and a spring.
We wind the spring
   when we turn the winding stem
   of the clock.
Listen to a clock.
You will hear a "tick tick."
As the spring unwinds
   the wheels turn, tick by tick.
As the wheels turn
   the hands move.
The hands point to the time.
Some clocks strike every hour
   or every quarter hour.
Our word clock
   is like the German word
   for bell, "glocke."
Old clocks had bells
   to tell the time.
Some small clocks
   do not strike.
We must watch their faces
   to tell the time.
We call some of them watches.
Some old clocks
   have falling weights
   instead of springs
   to turn their wheels.
Some clocks run by electricity.

Some clocks
   on clock towers
   are so big
   you can see them
   blocks away.
Their bells may
   strike the hour,
   BONG BONG BONG!
Some watches are so tiny
   they fit in a lady's ring.
You must hold them
   close to your ear
   to hear them tick.

cloth

Most of our clothes
  are made of cloth.
Our bed covers
  are made of cloth.
So are bath towels
  and many other things.
But what is cloth made of?
Cloth is woven from thread.
Cotton comes from
  the cotton plant.
Flax comes from a plant, too.
We call the cloth
  made from flax "linen."
Silk comes from the cocoons
  of silk worms.

It is unwound and spun
  into thread.
Rayon and nylon are made
  in factories.
Picture 1 shows
  a man fleecing a sheep
  to take off its wool.
He uses electric clippers
  like a barber's.
It does not hurt the sheep
  to lose its wool.
It soon grows more.

Flax **Cotton Plant**

Silk Worm

1

Picture 2 shows
  a woman
  spinning thread
  on an old spinning wheel.
The wool comes from sheep
  or from special goats.
Picture 3 shows
  a woman
  weaving cloth
  on a loom.
(Look up *weaving*.)

Thread is spun from wool
  or cotton
  or from flax or silk.
Or it is made by machine
  from other things.
Most cloth is woven
  in factories today.
Growers and spinners
  and weavers work
  to make us
  many kinds of cloth.

2

3

clothes

We wear clothes to protect us
  from rain or wind,
  from snow or cold,
  or from the sun's heat.

And we wear clothes
  to look nice.

We wear many different pieces
  of clothing.

Italy

Germany

Africa

Holland

Ireland

Japan

Mexico

In different places
   people may wear
      different kinds of clothes.
In icy lands
   they may wear furs and skins
      to keep them warm.
On the desert
   they may wear robes
      to keep the sun and wind
         from burning them.
They may wear
   light sandals
   or heavy boots
   on their feet.
Or they may wear
   fancy shoes.

They may wear clothes
   that take a lot
      of sewing.
Or they may wear clothes
   that are just wrapped
      around them
      and are not sewn at all.
In the hot jungles
   they may wear very little
      but beads and paint.
But everybody wears some
   sort of clothing.

cloud

Cumulus

Cirrus

Nimbostratus

Clouds float in the sky.
They are made of tiny drops
   of water or tiny crystals of ice
   gathered around
   tiny bits of dust.
Sometimes the tiny drops
   or crystals gather
   into bigger drops or flakes.

They fall from their clouds.
Then we have rain or snow.
(Look up *rain*.)
Clouds above us shut off
   the sunshine.
Then we have a cloudy day.
But up above the clouds
   the sun still shines.

coal

Coal is a black rock that burns.
It is found under the ground.
Men dig down to mine coal.
We call this a coal mine.

We call the men coal miners.
Coal is made
   from swampy forests
   of long, long ago.

Trees in these forests
   grew old and died.
The dead trees fell over.
The dead trees piled up there.
The land sank.
Mud washed over the forests.
They were buried.
Slowly, slowly they hardened
   into rock.
This black rock is coal.
Sometimes we find in coal
   the print of a fern.
That fern once lived
   in the forests of long ago.

coconut

Where the coconut palm grows,
   it gives people many things.
The huge leaves make roofs
   for homes.
The tall trunks make wood
   for building.
The tough fibers in the husks
   of the coconut fruits
   make coarse thread
   for ropes and cloth,
   baskets and mats.

fibers
husk
milk
meat

The coconut meat
   makes delicious food.
Oil pressed from coconut meat
   is good for cooking
   or making soap.
Its milk is good to drink.
The coconut palm
   is sometimes called
   "the tree of life."

color

Color can make things look either
   bright or dull.
Sunlight is made up of
   all the colors of the rainbow—

red
orange
yellow
green
blue
violet.

With three colors of paint
   red   blue   yellow
   you can make all the other colors.
Mix red and yellow.
You get orange.

Mix blue and yellow.
You get green.
Mix red and blue.
You get violet.
Colors help make things pretty!

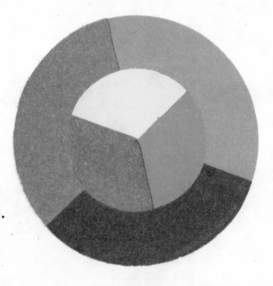

cooking

We fry bacon and eggs
  in a pan
  on the top of a stove
  or over a camp fire.
Most vegetables we cook.
We boil them
  in a little water
  in a pan
  over a hot fire.

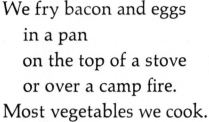

The heat of the boiling water
  cooks them.
Or we steam them
  over boiling water.
The hot steam cooks them.
We bake bread and rolls,
  cookies and cakes
  and pies
  in a hot oven.
Cooking is fun.
We get out a cook book
  to tell us how.
We get out bowls
  and spoons.
We get out all the food
  which we will need.
We mix
  and we stir.
Then we let things cook.
  And it tastes
  so good!

We cook most foods.
Some food we do not cook.
We like to eat them raw.
Fresh fruits and berries
  and some vegetables
  we like to eat raw.

But meat and eggs we cook.
We roast meat
  in a pan
  in a hot oven.
We broil meat
  on a rack
  close to a hot flame.

cork

We close bottles with corks.
We use cork pads
   under very hot dishes.
Water does not go through cork.
Heat does not go through cork
   well.
Cork comes from the bark
   of one kind of oak tree.
This tree is called the cork oak.

corn

Corn is a useful plant.
Cattle eat the stem
   and leaves
   of corn plants,
   chopped up.
The seeds of corn
   are called kernels.
They grow on stalks
   we call cobs.
We call cobs and kernels
   together an ear of corn.
Ears of corn are covered
   with green husks.
Sweet corn kernels
   are good to eat.

covered wagon

Families went West
   in covered wagons
   a hundred years ago.
They traveled in wagon trains.
The family took beds and chairs.
They took chests of clothes.
They took cooking pots and food.
They stored them all
   in their covered wagon
   for the long, long ride.
They said good-by
   to old friends.
They started for a new home.

dairy farm

On a dairy farm
cows are raised
for the milk they give.
A dairy farm may sell
all the milk from its cows.
It may take the cream
from some of the milk
and sell it.
It may make cheese
from some of the milk.
A dairy farm may make butter.
Then there is buttermilk
to sell, too.

Dairy cows need
a clean, airy barn.
In the summer they need
good pastures.
They must have good food
in winter, too.
Winter food is stored
in round silos near the barn.
The food in the silos is made
of green corn chopped up.
Dairy cows are carefully
brushed and washed
before they are milked.
Most dairy farms
have milking machines.
They have machines to take
the cream from the milk.
They have machines to keep
the milk cans clean.
A good dairy farm
is spic and span.

dam

A dam is a wall built
  across a river or stream.
The dam holds back the water.
It may make the water
  form a pond or lake.
Beaver dams form ponds.
Beavers build their dams
  of twigs and mud.
(Look up *beaver*.)
Men build their dams
  of concrete and steel
  or of hard-packed earth
  and rock.
Dams keep streams and rivers
  from causing floods.

Dams furnish water power
  to help make electricity.
(Look up *water*.)
A lake formed by a dam
  is called a reservoir.
People may swim in it.
They may go boating on it.
They may camp beside it.
The reservoir may furnish water
  for houses and factories
  in towns and cities
  round about.
It may furnish water to farms
  for livestock
  and for growing crops.
There are dams as tall
  as skyscrapers.
Some dams are beautiful.

dance

Music can
  make us feel
  like dancing.
Being happy can make us
  want to dance and sing.
All over the world
  people dance.

Mostly they dance
  to have a good time.
Some dances people do
  are dances from long ago.
There are dances to say
  "Thank you" to God
  for a good harvest.

There are dances
  to ask for rain
  or for help in a hunt
  to get food.

A dance may tell a story.
The dancers act out the story.

Each movement of the arms
  and hands and eyes
  may have a special meaning.
A dancer may spend years
  learning some dances.

Most dances need music.

The dancers wear
  fancy costumes.
They may be very beautiful.
Almost everyone likes to dance.

The dancer may make
  part of the music
  or beat time to the music.
The dancer may rattle a gourd
  or click castanets
  or tap metal shoe tips.
At shows we often see dancing
  on the stage.

And everywhere in the world
  people like watching
  lively or beautiful dancing.

day and night

It is light in the daytime.
It is dark at night.
Our light comes from the sun.

The sun can shine on
only half of the earth
at a time.
The half the sun is shining on
has day.
The other half has night.
The earth spins like a top.

Every part of the earth
keeps whirling in and out
of the sunlight.
Every part of the earth
has day and then night
over and over and over again.
Nighttime is cooler
than daytime
because the sun is not shining
on the night side of the earth.

Many creatures sleep
in the nighttime.
Others come out
to hunt for food.
For most people
nighttime is the time
for sleep and rest.

The first pale light of day
    we call dawn.
Soon, the sun comes up
    in the eastern sky.

The sun rises higher and higher
    in the east all morning.
It is highest at noon.
Shadows are short at noon.

When noon is past,
    the sun begins to go down
    in the western sky.
All afternoon it sinks
    lower and lower.
Shadows grow longer.
At last the sun sets.
Colors fade from sight.
First it is twilight.
Then it is night.

dentist

A dentist looks after teeth.
He straightens crooked teeth.
He fills holes in teeth.
We call these holes cavities.
He pulls out loose teeth.
If a grownup has a bad tooth
    the dentist may pull it out
    and make a new one
    to go in its place.
A dentist helps us
    keep our teeth clean
    and healthy.
A dentist is a good friend
    to have.

desert

A desert is land
   where not many plants
   can grow.
Many deserts are hot and sandy.
Very little rain falls.
Winds blow the dry sand about.
(Look up *sand*
   and *storm*.)

Some of the plants
   that can grow in deserts
   have no leaves.
Plants lose moisture
   from leaves.
Some have thick stems
   that store up water.
Some have thick leaves.
A desert plant may have
   beautiful flowers.
(Look up *cactus*.)

Cactus

Camels

Gila monster

Bull snake

Collared lizard

Kangaroo rat

Some desert animals do not need
water to drink.
They get the water they need
from the food they eat.
The kangaroo rat almost never
takes a drink.
Some desert animals
are especially fitted
for moving over hot sand.
Camels have padded feet.
(Look up *camel.*)
Some people live in deserts.
Many desert people
move from place to place.

We say they are nomads.
They must keep moving
to find food for themselves
and for their flocks.
These people can find water
where no stranger could.
They can find their way
without roads
across their bare lands.
Some deserts have special
green "islands."
There are wells and trees.
These places are called oases.
Desert people travel far
to get to an oasis.

Goats

Oasis

Bedouin tent

dew

At night the ground cools off.
Grass and flowers and toys
   left out get cooler, too.
When warm, moist air
   touches the cool things,
   some of its moisture
   forms drops of dew on them.
The dewdrops glisten
   in the cool morning.
But as the sun gets warmer,
   the dewdrops vanish.
The warm air takes up
   the moisture again.

diamond

A diamond is a very hard stone.
It is harder than iron,
   harder than steel.
A diamond is harder
   than anything else.
It can slice through glass
   and through metal.
Big clear diamonds cut to shape
   are glittering jewels.

dinosaur

The biggest animals
   that ever lived on land
   were dinosaurs.
But not all dinosaurs were huge.
Some were small as roosters,
   and some were middle-sized.
Some dinosaurs ate meat.
They had sharp teeth and claws.
Some dinosaurs ate plants.
Many of these had armor.
The really huge dinosaurs
   spent most of the time
   in swamps and ponds.
The water helped take
   their weight off their feet.

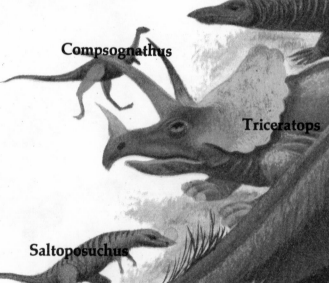

Compsognathus

Triceratops

Saltoposuchus

There were dinosaurs
    on the earth
    for millions and millions
    of years.
But millions of years ago
    the last of them disappeared.
Only small members
    of their reptile family
    are living today.
(Look up *reptile*.)

D

Tyrannosaurus rex

Stegosaurus

Diplodocus

dish

We eat from dishes.
We use flat plates.
We use round bowls.
We drink from cups
    set on saucers.
Our mothers have
    many dishes—
    platters for meat,
    vegetable dishes,
    salad bowls and gravy boats.

Most dishes are made of clay.
They have a smooth finish
    called a glaze.
They have pretty patterns, too.
Some have ground bone
    mixed with the clay
    to make them very hard.
Some dishes are plastic.
Some are silver
    or pewter or tin.
They do not break.

diving
and diver

At most swimming pools
    there are diving boards.
From them divers plunge down
    into the water.
If he does it right,
    a diver goes into the water
    smoothly.

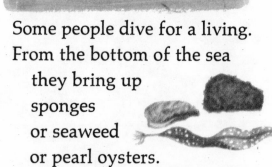

Some people dive for a living.
From the bottom of the sea
    they bring up
    sponges
    or seaweed
    or pearl oysters.
A skin diver may dive for fun.
He wears fins on his feet.
He wears a mask on his face.
He may have a snorkel
    to breathe through,
    or carry oxygen on his back.

Some divers go
   deep down
   in the sea.
They dive
   from
   a ship.
Deep-sea
   divers
   wear heavy suits
   with very heavy shoes
   to keep them upright.
They see through windows
   in their helmets.
Air is pumped down to them
   from the ship
   through rubber tubes.
Explorers in hollow steel balls
   have gone far deeper
   than any diver.
They have gone down
   to the deepest spot
   we know of in the sea
   to explore the cold, dark
   sea world there.

doctor

A doctor is a good friend.
When we are sick in bed,
   he comes to see us.
He helps us
   get well.

We go to see him
   at his office
   from time to time
   for checkups.
He measures to see
   how fast we are growing.
He gives us shots
   to keep us well.
Sometimes a shot pricks
   for a minute.
But we do not cry.
Only babies cry.
We know the doctor
   is not hurting us on purpose.
(Look up *hospital*
   for more about doctors.)

dog

Mongrel

For thousands of years
    people have had dogs.
Dogs make good companions.

Wolf

Fox

The wolf and the fox
    are cousins of the dog.
Some dogs look
    like wolves or foxes.

Great Dane

Irish setter

Boxer

Manchester terrier

Other dogs look very different.
Dogs are trained
    to do many kinds of work.

Bloodhounds

Some help by finding people
    who are lost.

English setter

Some help by finding game birds
    and other animals
    for hunters.
Some help as watchdogs.

Collie

Some help on farms and ranches
    by herding sheep and cattle.

Fox terrier

Whippet

Chihuahua

Skye

Gentle, playful dogs
    make good pets for children.

Dogs can run fast.
And they can swim.
They are slow swimmers.
Dogs can learn to do tricks.
They can sit up and beg.
They can balance on one leg
    or do a dance.
They can climb ladders
    and jump through hoops.
Dogs are very intelligent.
They bark and wag their tails
    to make us understand.
It seems sometimes that dogs
    can almost talk.

D

Poodle

doll

Dolls are playthings
   made to look like people.
Sometimes a doll is almost
   like a real live friend.
We can hug it and talk to it
   and play house with it.
We may have whole families
   of little dolls to play with.

We may have a dollhouse
   with tiny furniture in it.
A doll may be made
   of rubber, plastic
   or cloth.

A doll may be made
   of wood, leather
   or even corncobs.

drum

You can make a fine sound
   by beating a drum.
You can beat it to mark time
   for marching or for dancing.
It was long, long ago
   that people
   first stretched skins
   over hollow logs
   and beat out
   rhythms
   with their hands.
Jungle tribes still send news
   through the forest
   by beating on drums.
Today we have big drums
   and small drums
   in our bands and orchestras.
Usually we beat a drum
   with drumsticks.
Drumsticks are made of wood.
Some have wool or leather
   on the ends.
Drummers in orchestras
   and dance bands may have
   whole sets of drums to play.

eagle

An eagle is a big bird.
It hunts fish
    and other small animals
    to eat.
It nests on cliffs or in treetops.
The bald eagle appears
    on the seal of the
    United States of America.

It was chosen
    as the national bird
    because it is strong
    and swift and bold.

ear

We hear with our ears.
The part of an ear we see
    is called
    the outer ear.

Some animals have no ears.
And some animals with ears
    have ears we cannot see.
A bird's ears are hidden
    by feathers.
Some insects have ears
    on their legs.
Crickets do.
Some insects have ears
    under their wings.
Some moths do.
Some insects hear
    with their feelers.
Mosquitoes do.
The parts of our ears
    called
    the middle ear
    and the inner ear
    are inside our heads.
The eardrum is part of
    the middle ear.
It is a thin sheet of skin.
Sounds striking it make it
    move fast to and fro
    like the head of a tiny drum.
Nerves in the inner ear
    send sound messages
    to our brains
    and we hear the sounds.
(Look up *body*.)

Outer ear

Anvil **Hammer**

Eardrum

earth

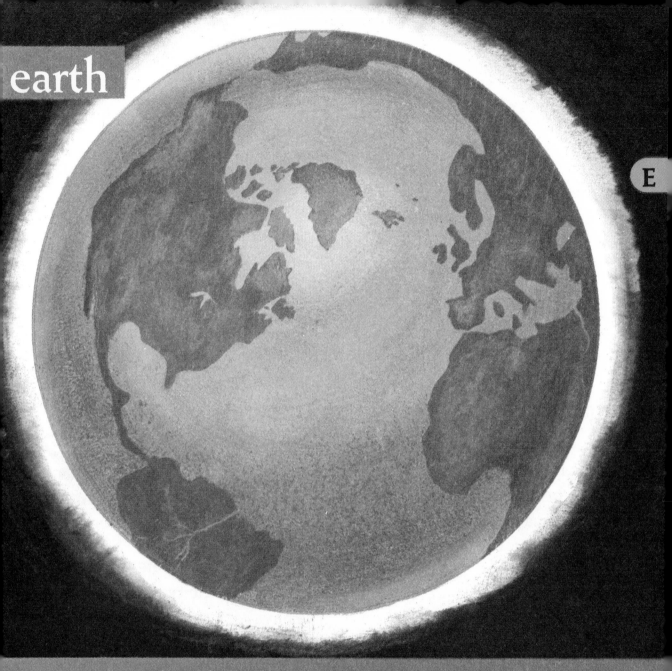

Our earth is a huge ball of rock
   wrapped in a blanket of air.
It travels around the sun.
It takes a year for the earth
   to make one trip.
The earth travels very fast.
But we do not feel it moving,
   for we are moving with it.

Our earth spins like a top, too.
We do not feel it spin, either.
The spinning gives us
   night and day.
(Look up *day and night*.)
Water covers much of the earth.
But more than half of all
   living things live on land.

electricity

Electricity gives us light.
Electricity gives us heat.
Electricity gives us power
   to do many kinds of work.
Most of us use electricity
   every day.

We may use an electric heater
   to warm a room quickly
   on cold mornings.
For breakfast
   we may have
   toast browned
   in an electric toaster.
Some of our mothers cook
   on electric stoves.
The coils get very hot.

In our homes
   we have electric lights.
Our mothers wash clothes
   in electric washers.
Electric motors
   swish the clothes around.

Electric dryers then dry them.
Hot electric irons
   press them smooth.
We have telephones
   and radios
   run by electricity.
We have television sets
   run by electricity, too.
We have
   electric record players.

We clean our houses
with vacuum cleaners.
They are run by electricity.
We may tell time
by electric clocks.
Electricity moves the hands
smoothly.
We may cool our homes
with electric fans
or air conditioners.

We keep our food cool
and fresh in refrigerators.

Many of them
are run by electricity.

Outside our homes
electricity helps us, too.
It lights our streets.
It runs traffic lights—
red for stop,
yellow for wait,
green for go.

It starts our cars
and gives them lights
at night.
It runs streetcars
and trolley buses.
It keeps airplanes
in touch with airports
by radio.
It runs many of the machines
in factories.
We say, "We could not do
without electricity!"
But in many parts of the world,
people do not have
electricity to help them.

elephant

The biggest animal on land
  is the elephant.
(Look up *whale*
  for the biggest in the sea.)
Elephants are at home
  in Africa and Asia.
Some live in other lands
  in circuses and zoos.
Asian elephants
  learn quickly.
They can be trained
  to do hard work.
An elephant can lift
  heavy things with its long,
  strong trunk.
An elephant uses its trunk
  to lift food to its mouth
  and to spray cool water
  over its back.

An elephant has two long teeth
  made of ivory.
They are called tusks.
An elephant uses its tusks
  as weapons
  and to dig for food.
(Look up *ivory*.)

elevator

An elevator takes us
  up or down
  in a tall building.
Cables pull it
  up and down
  in its shaft.
An elevator is run
  by electricity.

engine

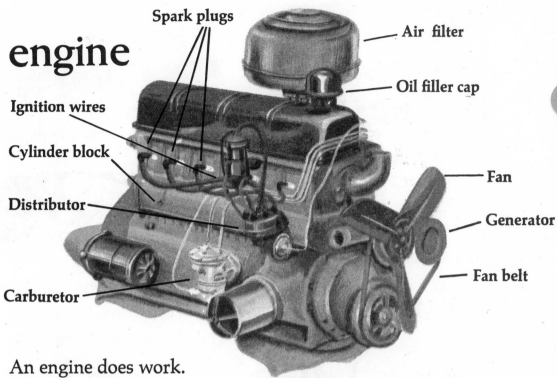

Spark plugs

Air filter

Oil filler cap

Ignition wires

Cylinder block

Distributor

Carburetor

Fan

Generator

Fan belt

An engine does work.
The engine
   of an automobile
   turns the wheels to make
   the automobile move.

Jet Engine

The engine
   of an airplane
   turns the propellers
   or shoots out jets of gas
   to make the plane move.
(Look up *aircraft*
   and *automobile*.)
A ship's engine turns
   propellers to push the ship
   through the water.

Gasoline is burned
   in an automobile engine
   to make it run.
We say that gasoline
   is the *fuel* used.
Gasoline is burned
   in an airplane engine, too.
Diesel engines,
   rocket engines,
   steam engines
   and steam turbines
   are other kinds of engines.
All of these are heat engines.
They all have to have
   some kind of fuel
   to make them
   do work for us.

Eskimo

Eskimos are nomads
  of the Far North.
They hunt and fish for food.
(Look up *Arctic, igloo, nomad,
  north, reindeer* and *umiak*.)

explorer

An explorer likes to visit
  new places
  and little-known people.
An explorer likes to learn
  new things.
Explorers first told us
  about the Eskimos
  and other
  people
  of faraway
  lands.

Explorers have sailed the seas.

Explorers have ridden camels
  across wide deserts.

Now explorers go high
  above the earth
  and deep down in the sea.
They learn new things.

eye

Lens
Iris

We see with our eyes.
We have eyelids
  to close our eyes.
We have eyelashes
  and tears to protect our eyes.
Eyelashes help keep out dust.
Tears wash dust away.
In our eyes there is a lens
  that helps us see clearly.
There is an iris to let light in
  and to shut light out.
There are other parts, too.
(Look up *body*
  and *lens*.)

factory

Many things we use
   are made by machine
   in a factory.
A factory must have power
   to keep its machines
   running.
(Look up *engine*.)
A factory must have workers
   to keep the machines
   running right.
A factory must have materials
   to work with.
If it is a dress factory
   it needs cloth and thread
   and patterns.
If it is a furniture factory
   it needs wood
   and nails
   and paint
   and varnish.
If it is an automobile factory
   it needs metal parts.

A factory must have an office.
It must have men there
   to plan the work
   and to sell
   what is made
   and to keep track
   of everything.
A factory must have
   a shipping department.
It must send out what it makes
   by truck
   or by train
   or by ship.
Many people work in factories.
A factory is a busy place.

fair

At a fair people show
   the best things
   they have made or grown.
At a county fair or state fair
   people show their best fruits
   and vegetables
   and farm animals.
They show grain and flour,
   jelly and jam,
   cakes and pies
   and sewing.
Prizes are given for the best.

At a trade fair
   machines
   and things made in factories
   are shown.
At a world's fair
   many countries show
   whatever they think is best
   about their country.
There are places to eat
   at a fair.
There are many things to see.
Often there are rides to take.
It is fun to go to a fair.

F

fairy

A fairy is a tiny, magical,
  make-believe creature.
Sometimes fairies are very good
  and helpful.
But they are often mischievous!

If we see dewdrops glisten
  on a cobweb on the grass,
  it may mean that fairies
  have been dancing there.
And though we know
  that fairies don't exist,
  it is fun to believe in them.

fairy tales

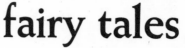

We read about fairies
  in fairy tales.
We all know Cinderella
  and her fairy godmother.
There are many tales
  with fairy creatures.
There are stories
  of brownies
  who work
  about the house.
There are stories
  of mischievous pixies.
There are stories
  of leprechauns
  who live under the ground.
They hide pots of fairy gold.

family

A family lives together
   in a home.
A family has a father.
Most fathers go to work
   almost every day.
A family has a mother.
Most mothers cook meals
   and look after the house.
Some mothers go to work.
Families may have children.
Children in the same family
   are called brothers and sisters.
Families have
      grandparents
      and they may have
      aunts and uncles and cousins.
These people are all related
   to each other.
They are called relatives.
A family works together.
Everyone in the family helps.

A family plays together
   sometimes.
They may go on picnics.
They may watch television
   or listen to music.

They may play games.
They may read together.
In families
      we learn to work and play
      and live together happily.
We learn the fun of doing things
   for others, in a family.

farm

Food is grown on a farm.
Some farms grow
   many kinds of food.
They may grow grains—
   corn and wheat.
They may raise animals
   for meat—
   cows and chickens,
   pigs and sheep.
They may grow vegetables—
   beans and peas,
   cabbage and squash.
They may have an orchard
   with fruit trees—
   apples, pears, peaches.
On such farms,
   there are many kinds
   of work.

Some farms raise
   just one crop.
A lemon grove may have
   just lemons.

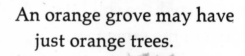

An orange grove may have
   just orange trees.

An olive grove may have
   just olive trees.

Some farms just raise cows
   to get milk and butter.
(Look up *dairy farm*.)
A cattle ranch raises
   just cattle.
It must have lots of land
   for them to graze.
It has cowboys to watch
   the herds.

(Look up *ranch*.)

Some farms raise
   just chickens or turkeys
   or ducks.
We call them poultry farms.
Some small farms raise
   just vegetables for market.
We call them truck farms.
We need many kinds of farms
   and farmers to raise our food.

fence

A fence shuts in a yard
   or a field.
It is a kind of wall.
Some old fences
   are made of split logs.
We call them rail fences.

Some fences are made of wire.

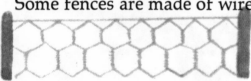

The wire may have barbs.

Barbs make it harder
   to go over or through
   the fence.
Some fences are made of stone.

A fence has a gate or a stile
   instead of a door.

fern

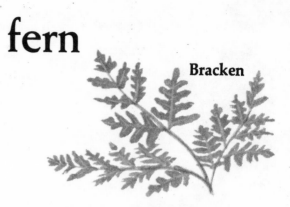

Bracken

A fern is a feathery plant.
A fern has roots,
   a stem, and leaves.
The leaves are called fronds.

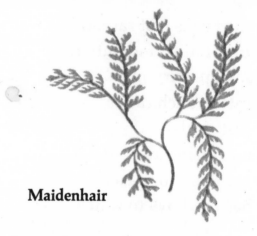

Maidenhair

But it has no flowers.
It has no seeds.
Instead of seeds,
   a fern grows tiny spores.
(Look up *mushroom*.)
The tiny spores fly on the wind.
They fall to the ground.
From them grow new plants.
These become tiny ferns.

Some ferns grow as tall as trees.
They grow best
where it is
very sheltered
and damp.

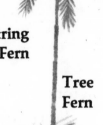

Shoestring Fern

Tree Fern

fingerprints

When you touch a surface,
  you leave fingerprints on it.
Sometimes they are hard to see,
  but they are always there.
The interesting thing
  about fingerprints
  is that no one else
  has fingerprints like yours.
Fingerprints are useful records.
Footprints are too.
Hospitals may make footprints
  of new babies.

fire

Fire burns. It is hot.
Its heat can cook food.

Fire can do work.
It makes engines run.
(Look up *engine.*)
Fire can also do harm.
It can burn a house.

It can burn a forest.

Fire can burn us.
And a burn hurts.
Even a small fire
  can grow large
  and do harm.
We must be very careful
  with fire.

fireman

Firemen fight fires.
When a fire starts,
   someone turns on an alarm.
It warns the firemen
   in the fire house.

They jump onto fire trucks
   and drive to the fire.
They sound sirens
   to tell cars
   to get out of their way.
They go fast.
For a fire can spread fast.

On lakes and rivers
   firemen may have fireboats.
Airplanes and parachutes help
   firemen get to forest fires.

Tractors are used
   to dig trenches
   around the fire
   to keep it from spreading.

Firemen do hard work.

fish

Fish live in water.
They swim about.
They steer with their fins.
They breathe through their gills.
Their gills take air
   from the water.

Fish have eyes but no eyelids.
They have bones
   but no legs or arms.
They have blood,
   but it is not warm like ours.
Fish are cold-blooded animals.
Most fish lay eggs.
As soon as the eggs are laid
   they are left alone to hatch.
Fish do not care for their babies.
Very few fish hatch their eggs
   inside their bodies.

Some fish eat plants.
Many fish eat other fish.
Big ones eat small ones.
Still bigger ones eat big ones.
Some fish are small enough
   to fit in your hand.
Some grow larger than a man!
Some fish live in rivers.

Some fish live in lakes.

Many fish live in the oceans.

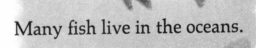

fishermen

Men who catch fish
   are called fishermen.
They try to catch fish
   that are good to eat.
Some fishermen go fishing
   for fun.
They may wade in a stream
   and throw out a line
   attached to a fishing rod.
This is called "casting."
They may sit on a bank
   with a fishing pole
   and a long string on it.
The string has a fish hook
   on the end.
Bait is put on the hook
   to attract the fish.
Bait may be a worm, a fly,
   or pieces of fish.

When a fish bites the bait
   the fisherman
   pulls in his string.
He has caught a fish!
Many fishermen fish from a boat.
It may be a row boat.
It may be a big sea-going boat.

The fishermen may be fishing
   for great big fish.
Many fishermen do not fish
   just for fun.
Many fishermen catch fish
   for a living.
Fishing is their job.
They live beside the sea.
They go far out to sea to fish.

The sea may be stormy.
They may get cold and wet.
Fishing is hard work.
But still they go.
Many fishermen
    whose work is fishing
    use nets to catch fish.
The nets have floats on one edge.
These floats are light.
They float on top of the water.
They keep the net from sinking.
The floats may be
    hollow glass balls.
Or they may be cork.
Fishermen look for fish
    swimming together.
We say the fish swim in schools.
A big school of fish
    makes a good catch.

The fishermen load their boats
    with fish from the nets.
Some fishermen build big traps.
They use a sort of basket.
The fish swim in.
They cannot swim out again.
The fishermen catch them.
There are many ways
    to catch fish.
Some fishermen use spears.
Some even use bows and arrows.
But still the big ones
    often get away.

fish hatchery

Some young fish are raised
    in fish hatcheries.
Fish eggs hatch there.
The young fish are fed
    and kept safe.
Then they are put into lakes
    and streams
        where fishermen like to fish.

flag

A flag is a kind of sign.
It is made of cloth.
It may stand for a country
  or a state
  or for some group.
Every country has a flag.
A country's flag deserves honor
  and respect from its people.
It flies over public buildings
  of that country.

The United Nations
  has a flag.
It stands for all the countries
  working together for peace.
A flag may give a message.
Each color stands
  for something.
Each pattern has a meaning.

The United States of America's
  flag is red, white and blue.
In the blue of the sky
  there is a star for each state.
The red and white stripes
  stand for the thirteen states
  which started the country.

Ships at sea use small flags
  to give news to other ships.
Sailors learn to read
  the language of flags.

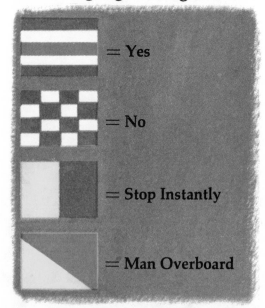

= Yes

= No

= Stop Instantly

= Man Overboard

flood

A flood is water
  covering land
  that is usually dry.
Too much rain can cause a flood.
Rivers rise.
The water goes over their banks.
A flood can be very serious.
The water covers roads.
It runs into towns and houses.
It destroys crops.
People must leave their homes.

A storm at sea may cause floods.
The water dashes over a sea wall.
Or it breaks a hole in the wall.
And a flood covers the land.

flour

Most flour is made from grain.
Grain seeds are ground up fine
  into powdery flour.
Plain flour used to be sold
  only in big sacks.
Now it can also be bought
  in packages already mixed
  for cakes, cookies, and bread.

flour mill

A flour mill is a big factory.
It has tall elevators to hold grain.
It has big rollers to grind grain
  into flour.
The flour is put into sacks.
It is shipped all over the country.

flower

Rose

The pretty part of a plant
   is usually the flower.
Many plants have flowers.
Flowers lead to seeds.
And seeds start new plants.
The apple blossom is the flower
   of the apple tree.
Without apple blossoms,
   an apple tree
   would never have apples
   with seeds inside.
What happens?
Bees fly to the apple blossom
   to suck its sweet juice.
Bees bring yellow pollen
   from another apple blossom.
The pollen rubs off on the pistil,
   a part of the apple blossom.
The pollen travels down
   inside the pistil.
And it starts seeds growing
   there.

Apple Blossom

Now the work of the blossom
   is done.
Its petals drop off.
The seed case grows and grows.

Apple

It becomes an apple.
Inside are the apple seeds.
From them new trees can grow.
Most trees have flowers.
Some are so small
   we do not notice them.
Vegetables have flowers.
We eat the flowers
   of cauliflower.
We eat the seeds
   of corn and peas and beans
   after the flowers are gone.

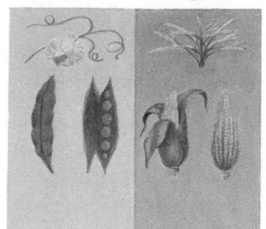

Some plants we grow
   not for food
   but just because the flowers
   are pretty.
In our gardens we grow
   many flowers—
   roses and daisies,
   sweet peas and pansies.

In the woods and meadows
   we find wild flowers.
We find pussy willows.
We find violets.
We find buttercups.
We find Queen Anne's lace
   and milkweed
   and dandelions.

Daisy

Iris

Violet

Tulip

Dandelion

Poppy

Lily
of the Valley

Buttercup

We grow hollyhocks and iris,
   poppies and lilies,
   tulips and lilies of the valley.
(Look up *garden*.)

Even in the desert flowers grow.
There are flowers in the jungle.
(Look up *desert* and *jungle*.)
There is hardly a place
   in the world
   where flowers do not bloom!

fog

Fog is a kind of cloud.
(Look up *cloud*.)
But fog is not high in the air,
   like most clouds.
Fog is close to the ground.
It feels damp around us.
Clouds are mostly water.
So is fog.
It is very hard to see through.
At sea there are fog horns.
They warn ships of rocks.

food

We need food
   every day.
Our bodies
   turn food
   and drink
   into bones
   and muscle
   and blood.
Food makes us grow.
It makes us strong.
It keeps us warm too.
Food is the fuel
   for our bodies' engines.
(Look up *engine*.)

We eat many different foods.
Our bodies need them.
Some fruits and nuts,
    fish and meat
    and vegetables
    come to us
    from far away.
They come by ship
    or train
    or truck.
But in many lands
    people eat
    just what grows near by.
Some people eat
    rice and fish
    almost every day.

Some people eat bananas
    for almost every meal.
Sometimes they have a little meat
    or vegetables too.
Some people eat mostly
    potatoes.
Some eat mostly corn meal
    and beans.
They make flat corn-meal bread.
They roll up the beans
    in the bread.
Most of us try to have
    some milk, some meat,
    some fruit and vegetables,
    some bread and cereal
    every day.

forest

A forest has many trees.
Trees give us wood.
We use wood for many things.
We use wood to build houses
    and furniture.
(Look up *lumbering*.)
We use wood to make paper,
    cellophane and tools.
Some medicines are made
    from wood.
We burn wood for fuel.
Forests are important.
They are beautiful too.
Forests give us quiet shade.
They give homes to animals
    and birds.
Lumbermen used to spoil
    many forests.

They cut down all the trees.
Now they are more careful.
They plant new trees
    when they cut some down.

Forest fires spoil many forests.
We must be very careful
    in forests
    not to start a fire!
In very hot, wet lands,
    rain forests or jungles grow.
(Look up *jungle*
    and *tree*.)

fossil

A fossil is all that remains
of a long-ago animal
or plant.
We find fossils in rocks.
They may be footprints.

They may be bones
or patterns of leaves.
Fossils tell us something
about life long, long ago.

fountain

A fountain has water
spurting up out of it.
A fountain looks cool.
It sounds pleasant.
Many fountains are beautiful, too.

fruit

Some fruits are sweet.
Some fruits are good to eat.
They have seeds inside.
Some fruits have one seed.
Apricots,
peaches
plums
cherries
and avocado pears
have only one seed.
Some fruits have more seeds.
Watermelons and
other melons do.

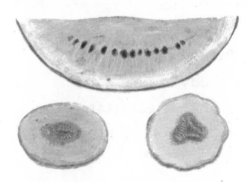

furniture

We use furniture in our homes.
We sit on chairs.

Most grapes, apples, oranges,
    lemons and grapefruit
    have many seeds.
So do pears and persimmons
    and dates and figs.

We eat from tables,
    and put things on them.

Bananas have only dots
    where their seeds used to be.
Some berries are very seedy.

We sleep on beds.

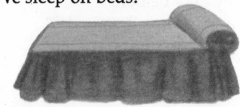

We keep clothes and supplies
    in chests and cupboards.

Strawberries
    and raspberries
    and gooseberries are.
But seedy or not,
    we like to eat fruit.
And fruit is good for us.

We have desks to write at.
We have television sets
    and lamps.

There are many kinds
of furniture.
The kind we have depends
on where and how we live.

For cold, drafty houses
people used to have
chairs with sides
to keep off the cold.

They had beds with curtains
to draw.

Some people built beds
in wall cupboards!

F

People have little furniture
in Japan.
They unroll mats or carpets
to sleep on.

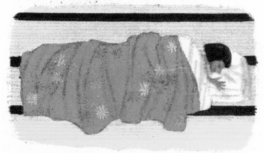

They roll up their "beds"
during the day.
They do not care for chairs
like ours.

They sit on mats or on the floor.
Their tables are very low.
All the people have
their own ideas of how
to make a home comfortable.

fur

Seal

Many animals have coats of fur.
Fur is very thick hair.
People who live
where it is cold
like to wear coats
made of animal fur.
A fur coat is soft and warm.
Some people like to wear
fur coats
just to look nice.
Mink, beaver, seal,
muskrat, fox and rabbit
are some animals
which are raised or hunted
because people like
to wear their fur.

Mink

Fox

Beaver

Rabbit

game

We play games.
Some games we play
    out-of-doors.
All kinds of hide-and-seek
    and tag
    and other running games
    we play out-of-doors.

When there is fresh snow
    we can play fox-and-geese.
On a sidewalk
    we can play hopscotch.
We mark the sidewalk
    with chalk for it.
Some games are played
    on special fields.
Baseball is played
    on a baseball diamond.
Tennis is played
    on a tennis court.
Golf is played
    on a golf course.
Football is played
    on a football field.

Cards

Checkers

Hide-and-Seek

Tag

Hopscotch

Golf

Football

Baseball

Tennis

Some games we play
     in the house.
Many indoor games we play
     sitting down.
We may play on a board.
We may play
     with counters
     of ivory, wood or plastic.

Dominoes   Cards

We may play with cards.
There are many, many games
     to play.
In a game
     we do our best to win.
Sometimes we do win.
And sometimes we lose.
Some games we play alone.
Some games we play
     with one other person.
Some games we play
     with several others.
And some we play with teams.
We need teams for baseball
     and football.
Games are fun to play.
Even quiet word games
     are fun.

G

garden

We grow plants in gardens.
Some gardens are large
  and beautiful.
They may have green lawns
  and beds of flowers
  and paths to walk on.
They may have pools of water
  for water plants and fish.
They may have
  fountains
  and birdbaths.
They may have trees
  and bushes and hedges.
A big garden may have
  a little garden house
  where people can sit.

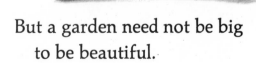

But a garden need not be big
  to be beautiful.

A garden with a careful **pattern**
  is called a formal garden.

A garden with plants
  growing among rocks
  is called a rock garden.
A garden with flowers grown
  to be cut for bouquets
  is called a cutting garden.
A garden with vegetables
  of different kinds
  is called a vegetable garden.

Every garden
  has some plants.
Every garden needs water
  to make the plants grow.
Rain is good for a garden.
If there is not enough rain,
  a garden hose
  or sprinklers help.

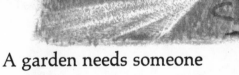

A garden needs someone
  to work in it,
  to keep it looking nice.

gardener

People who work in gardens
  are called gardeners.
They may do it as their job.

They may do it for the love
  of seeing things grow.
Gardeners have a lot to do.
They have to prepare the soil.
They have to plant seeds
  or set out young plants.
They must pull up weeds
  or chop them out with a hoe.
They must keep insects
  from eating the plants.
They must water the plants.
It is a fine thing
  to make a garden grow.

ghost

A ghost is
   a make-believe creature.
It comes out at night.
When people hear
   a strange noise at night
   they may say,
"It sounds like a ghost!"
It is fun to dress as a ghost
   on Halloween.
There are many stories
   about ghosts.
We call them ghost stories.

giant

A giant is a great big man
   in storybooks.
There are many stories
   about giants.
No real people are as big
   as giants in storybooks.

But sometimes a man
   grows taller than most.
We may call him
   a giant of a man.
He seems somewhat
   like the giants in stories.

If a tall giraffe wants to drink
  or to eat some grass,
  it must spread its legs wide.
Then its mouth can reach
  the water or low grass.
A giraffe can run fast
  on its long legs.
It can kick hard
  with its hoofs.
This big animal
  has almost no
  voice at all.

giraffe

A giraffe is an animal
  with a very long neck.
It has long legs, too.
It eats leaves from treetops.

glacier

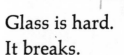

A glacier is a huge mass
   of slowly moving ice.
It may be a river of ice
   in high mountains.
It may be a great sheet of ice
   in a very cold land.
A glacier is formed
   when a great deal of snow
   falls year after year
   and does not melt away.
The snow piles up.
It packs hard and turns to ice.
(Look up *ice*.)
As the ice gets thicker
   and thicker,
   the glacier starts to move.
It moves too slowly for us to see.
Long, long ago glaciers covered
   much of our land.
Then they melted away.
But we can still see
   lakes and valleys they carved
   and hills they piled up.

glass

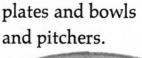

Glass is hard.
It breaks.
We can usually see through it.
Window glass keeps rain out.
It lets sunlight in.
We drink from glasses.
We may have dishes of glass—
   plates and bowls
   and pitchers.

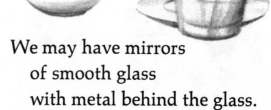

We may have mirrors
   of smooth glass
   with metal behind the glass.
Instead of seeing
   through a glass mirror
   we see ourselves!

Sometimes we wear
   glass goggles
   to protect our eyes.

Many people wear eyeglasses
   to see things better.
The glass in them is not flat.
It is specially shaped
   to help a person see.
A piece of glass so shaped
   is called a lens.
Light bulbs are made of glass.
So are most bottles.
(Look up *lens.*)

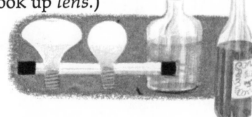

Glass is made of sand
   with certain things added.
The sand must be heated
   until it melts.
The sand has to be made
   very, very hot
   before it melts.

So the furnace must be
   very, very hot to make glass.
Some glass is blown.
A melted lump is picked up
   on the end of a hollow rod.
A man blows into the rod.
The glass bubbles out
   like a balloon.
A skillful man can give
   the glass any shape
   as he twirls the rod.
Glass can also be colored.
Some beautiful windows
   are made of small bits
   of colored glass
   put together with lead.
We call these
   stained glass windows.

globe

A globe is round.
It is round like the earth.
It shows us the lands and seas
of the earth.
We can find our own country
on a globe.
We can find other countries,
too.

goat

A goat can live in rocky lands
where there is
not much grass.
A goat can find something
to eat almost anywhere.
Some goats give good milk.
Some goats give fine wool.

gold

Gold is a bright yellow metal.
It is rather soft.
Not much gold is found.
And many people want it.
So it costs a great deal.

Gold is used for jewelry
and for beautiful ornaments.
It used to be used for coins.
We have no gold money today.
But the country has bars of gold
stored away.
One bar of gold
is worth a great deal.

Gold is found in rocks.
Sometimes water washes
    bits of gold out of the rock.
The gold is washed down
    a river.
Gold hunters may find the gold
    by digging up sand and gravel
    from the river bed.
They put it in a flat pan
    and wash away
    the sand and gravel.
The gold is left in the pan.
This way of getting gold
    is called panning for gold.
But most gold is dug
    out of the rock.
Miners go deep underground.
A gold mine may be
    more than a mile deep.

grape

Grapes grow in bunches
    on vines.
Many grapevines
    make a vineyard.
There are vineyards
    in many lands.
Most grapes are purple
    or green.

Fresh grapes are good to eat.
They are sweet and juicy.
From them we make
    grape juice and jelly,
    jam and wine.
Dried grapes are good, too.
We call dried grapes raisins.

G

grass

Lawn grass makes our lawns
green and pretty.
Horses, sheep and cows eat
meadow grasses.

Rice, oats and wheat are grasses.
The seeds of these grasses
give us flour and cereals.
Another grass gives us sugar.
It is sugar cane.

greenhouse

A greenhouse is a house of glass
for growing plants.

It may be cold outside.
But inside a greenhouse
the air is warm.

Sunshine warms the air.
A heater inside may help, too.
In the warm, damp air
of the greenhouse
plants from hot lands
can grow in snowy winter.

gypsy

Gypsies wander
over the countryside.
Their homes used to be
bright-colored wagons
pulled by horses.
In some countries
gypsies still live in wagons.
But in the United States
most gypsies have cars
and trailers now.
Gypsies like bright colors
and sad songs
and going their own way.

hair

We have hair on our heads.
We have finer, softer hair
on our bodies.

Many animals have thick hair
we call fur or wool.

hand

A hand has five fingers.
One is called a thumb.
It is the thumb
that gives a hand
a really firm grip.

With our fingers and thumbs
we can lift and hold
and do all sorts of things.

harbor

A harbor is where boats
and ships come in to shore.
A good harbor protects boats
and ships from the storms
of the open sea.
Men build sea walls
called breakwaters
to help make harbors quiet.
Then boats and ships
can load and unload easily.

hat

We wear hats or caps
    to keep off rain and sun.
We wear them for warmth, too.
And we wear them to look nice.
Some people wear
    hats or caps
    that tell what they do.

Sailors
    and baseball players
    have special hats or caps.

So do policemen
    and firemen
    and cowboys.

Here are some ways
    people shade their heads
    when the sun is hot.

heart

A valentine heart says,
    "I love you."
People used to think
    love and bravery
    came from the heart.
Now we know they do not.
But certainly your heart
    is very important.
It is the engine
    which pumps the blood
    through your body.
(Look up *blood*.)
Without that pump
    you could not live.
Put your fingertips
    on your wrist.
You can feel the pumping there.
It is called your pulse.
To see how big your heart is,
    double up your hand.

Your fist is about the size
    of your heart.

helicopter

A helicopter
    flies without wings.
It has a huge propeller on top—
    or sometimes two.
The propeller of a helicopter
    is called a rotor.
A helicopter can fly
    straight up or down
    as well as ahead.
It does not need a big airport
    to land on.

highway

A highway is a main road.
(Look up *road*.)
Some highways are very busy.
Many, many cars and trucks
    travel on them.
A driver on the highway
    must know the rules
    of the highway.
We call these traffic rules.
(Look up *traffic*.)

He must not go too fast or slow.
He must watch out for other cars.
Some busy highways
    have cloverleaf crossings.
Do you see the four-leaf clover
    in the picture?
It is for safety.
You never have to cross
    in front of other cars.
You can change
    to the other highway
    and go in either direction
    by making right turns only.
Or you can cross over or under it.
A highway has places to eat
    and to sleep along it.
There may be a shopping center
    on a highway near a town.

hill

A hill is land that is higher
    than the land around it.
We can climb a hill.
Sometimes we can see
    a long way from a hilltop.
But a hill is not as high
    as a mountain.

hippopotamus

A hippopotamus spends
    much of its time in water.
It eats mainly water plants.
It is a very large animal.
Of all four-legged animals
    only the elephant is larger.

history

History is the story of the past.
It is the story of all the people
    who have lived.
It tells us how they lived.
Their lives were different
    from ours in many ways.
History is not make-believe.
Its stories are true.
They are interesting to read.
Some day the story of how
    we live will be history, too.

holiday

Holiday means "holy day."
Some holidays are holy days
  of a religion.
Christmas is one.

Christmas is celebrated
  with gifts,
  with lighted trees,
  with songs
  and parties,
  and in Christian
  churches.

Easter is another holiday
  of the Christian religion.
Easter is celebrated
  with colored eggs
  and candies,
  and in Christian
  churches.

Different religions
  have different holidays.
Hanukkah is the Jewish Festival
  of Lights.
Hanukkah lasts
  for eight days.
It is celebrated with gifts
  and in the temple.

Dewali is a holiday of lights
  celebrated in India.
Small clay lamps are lighted
  all around the houses.
Dewali is a holy day
  in the Hindu religion.
Some holidays
  are history days.

We celebrate the birthdays
  of great men.
We celebrate the first harvest
  in our land with Thanksgiving.

We celebrate the founding
    of our country
    on the Fourth of July.

We have picnics and parades.
Most people do not work
    on holidays.
We have fun on holidays.
You have your own holiday.
You celebrate it every year.
Maybe you have a party.
You invite your friends.
You play games.
You have ice cream and cake.
You open presents.
Do you know
    what your holiday is?
It is your birthday.
Happy birthday to you!

horse

Horses can run fast.
Some run in races.

Some horses pull heavy loads.
Some help in hunting.
They can jump high.

Horses can learn to do tricks.
But the nicest thing
    about a horse
    is this:
    It will
    take you
    for a ride
    on its back.

hospital

You may go to a hospital
    when you are sick.
A hospital has doctors
    and nurses.
A nurse smooths your bed.
She brings your meals.
She makes you feel better.
Your doctor may say
    you need an operation.
Then you go
    to a big, bright room.
You are put to sleep
    so that the operation
    will not hurt you.
Everyone in a hospital
    tries to help you get well.

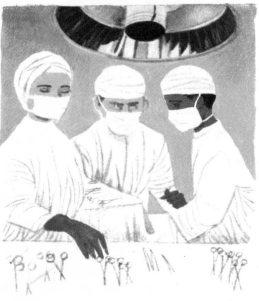

In a hospital you have
    a wonderful bed.
It cranks up and down.
You can have your head up.
You can sit up to eat.

Or down you go flat for a nap.
You can even have
    your feet or knees up!

Sometimes a lady
    comes to your room
    with toys on a cart.
You may borrow them to play.
If you have a roommate,
    you each have a bed.
You each have a night table.
You each have a chair
    for visitors to sit on.
When you get up
    and dress to go home,
    everyone says, "Good-bye."
A hospital is such
    a friendly place to go.

140

hotel

Some hotels are called motels.
"Motel" means "motor hotel."

A hotel has bedrooms
    for people away from home
    to sleep in.
A hotel has a dining room
    for people to eat in.
It has a kitchen
    where meals are cooked.
It has sitting rooms.
A big hotel has shops
    where you can buy things.
It has a barber shop.
On some lakes and seashores
    and in other beautiful spots
    there are hotels
    we call resort hotels.
People go to these hotels
    to spend their vacations.

You can drive your car
    right into a motel.
You park it
    right beside your room.
It is handy whenever you want
    to start off again.
Some motels have
    swimming pools.
Some have pretty lawns
    and gardens.
Some have dining rooms.
They all have bedrooms
    with bathrooms.
When you have been
    riding in a car all day,
    it is nice to clean up
    and jump into bed.

house

You live in a house.
It may be an apartment house
in a city.

You may live in a house
on wheels in a trailer park.
But wherever you live is home.
Houses may be built
of many different things.
(Look up *buildings*.)
What your house is made of
depends partly on where it is.

Many families may live
in one apartment house.
Your house may be a farmhouse
in the country.
You may not be able to see
any other house from yours.
You may live in a house
in a village or town.
Your friends may live
in houses down the street.

If it is on stony land,
it may be made of stone.

If it is in a country
with lots of trees, your house
may be made of wood.

If there is lots of clay around
    a house may be made
    of mud or mud bricks.

People who live in deserts
    and move around a lot
    may have a tent for a house.
It will be made of cloth
    woven from the wool
    of sheep and goats.

People who live on low land
    near water
    may have houses made
    of grass and reeds.

People who live on big rivers
    may have floating houses
    built on rafts.
They may even live in boats!

The important thing
    about a house
    is that a family
    lives there together.
That is what makes a house
    a home.

hummingbird

A hummingbird is very tiny.
It can fly very fast.
Its wings move so fast
    that it can stand still
    in the air.

A hummingbird drinks nectar,
    the sweet juice in flowers.
It barely opens its long beak.
Its tongue flicks out
    from the end of the beak.
A hummingbird builds
    a tiny, soft nest.
Its white eggs are no bigger
    than peas.

One hummingbird we see
    often is the ruby-throated.
In the sunlight
    its throat glows like jewels.
In the warmer parts
    of North and South America
    other hummingbirds live.
Some have fancy head crests
    or collars of feathers
    or marvelous long tails.
Here are a few of them.

ice

Ice is frozen water.
It is cold and hard.
If ice gets warm, it melts.
It turns back to water.
We use ice to keep
    foods and drinks cold.
Fresh foods keep better
    when we store or ship them
    if they are cold.

People used to get
    all their ice
    from frozen lakes or ponds
    in winter.
Now we can make ice
    in refrigerators
    and in ice plants
    all year round.

An iceman used to load
    blocks of ice
    on his wagon.

He drove around the town.
If a customer
    wanted 50 pounds
    of ice,
    "50" was at the top
    of a card
    in a window.
The iceman had ice tongs
    as long as your arm.
With his tongs he picked up
    a 50-pound block.
He carried it into the house
    and put it in the icebox.

In some places
    people still use iceboxes.
But most of our homes
    have mechanical refrigerators
    to keep foods cold.

iceberg

An iceberg is a mountain of ice.
It floats in the sea.
Most of an iceberg
    is under water.
An iceberg
    comes from a glacier.
(Look up *glacier*.)
A glacier is a slow-moving
    sheet or river of ice.
When a glacier meets the sea,
    huge chunks of ice break off.
They are icebergs.

ice cream

Ice cream is cold and sweet.
Ice cream is good to eat.
Ice cream is made
    of milk or cream,
    sugar and flavorings.
As it grows cold,
    it gets thick.
It must be stirred
    to keep big ice crystals
    from forming.
Stirring keeps it creamy.
Most people like ice cream.
Most children like it very much.

ice skate

Ice skates are for skating
    on ice.
They have thin steel blades
    on the bottom.
They glide smoothly
    over the ice.
But first you must learn
    to stand on them.

igloo

An igloo is an Eskimo house
    made of hard snow blocks.
An Eskimo can build
    an igloo very fast.

He lives in it in winter
    when he is hunting.

A little tunnel doorway
    keeps the cold wind out
    and the warm air in.
A whale oil lamp
    gives light and heat.
An igloo is very warm.

Indian

The Indians lived in America
    before the "palefaces" came.
There were many different
    Indian tribes.
Some lived on our open plains.
They hunted the buffalo.
Buffalo skins
    made their tepees.
Buffalo skins
    made robes and clothes.
Buffalo meat gave them food.

We call them Plains Indians
    or "people of the buffalo."

Some Indians lived
    in the warm, dry Southwest.
They built villages of stone
    or sun-dried mud.
We call the villages pueblos.
A pueblo was like
    a big apartment house
    several stories high.
There were outside ladders
    for getting from one story
    to another.
At the foot of the village
    were fields of corn,
    squash, beans and cotton.
Pueblo Indians made pottery
    and jewelry.
They wove beautiful cloth.
We call their ancestors
    the Cliff Dwellers.
(Look up *cliff dwellers*.)

Some Indians lived
    in our eastern woodlands.
They built long houses of wood.
They made canoes of birch bark.
These woodland Indians
    hunted and fished.
They grew corn and beans,
    squash and tobacco.
Out of seashells
    they made money
    called wampum.

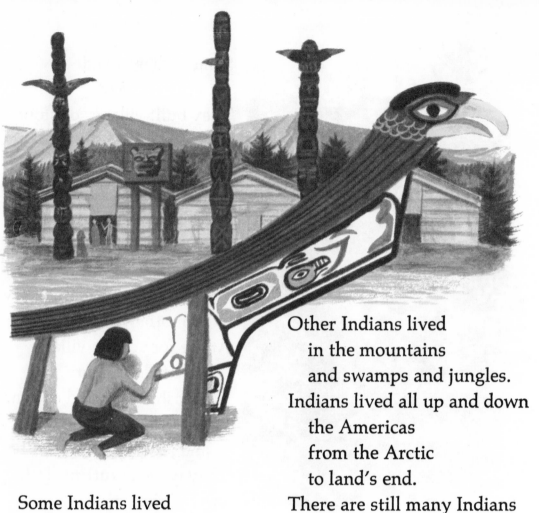

Other Indians lived
in the mountains
and swamps and jungles.
Indians lived all up and down
the Americas
from the Arctic
to land's end.
There are still many Indians
living in America.
Many of those in North America
live on reservations.

Some Indians lived
in the Northwest
along the seashore.
They made fine boats.
They built wooden houses.
They made tall poles
carved and painted
with animals.
We call the poles
totem poles.
These Indians
were skilled fishermen.
They fished with hooks
and spears and nets.

ink

We often write or draw
   with pen and ink.
Lines made with ink
   last a long time.
Ink marks are hard to erase.
We must be more careful
   with pen and ink
   than with pencil.
Ink comes in many colors.

insect

Insects have six legs.
No other animals
   are six-legged.
There are thousands
   and thousands
   of kinds of insects.

Housefly

Buckeye Butterfly

There are bees and bugs
   and butterflies.
There are ants
   and silverfish
   and beetles.

Walkingstick

There are wasps and moths
   and walking sticks.
There are many others besides.
(Look up *bee* and *beetle*
   and *bug* and *butterflies*.
Also look up *wasp*.)
Every grown-up insect has
   a pair of feelers.

Lubber Grasshopper

Every one has a wonderful
   waterproof coat, too.
An insect's waterproof coat
   is made of a tough material
   called chitin.
Most insects have wings.

Many have two pairs.
Beetles do.
A beetle has a pair of hard
    wings on top.

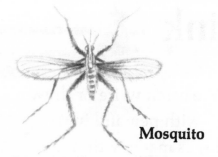

Mosquito

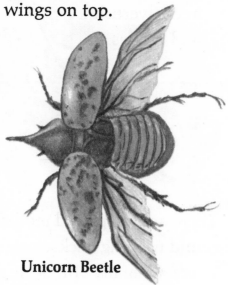

Unicorn Beetle

Neither do lice or fleas.
Worker ants and termites
    have no wings.

Silverfish

It has a pair of soft wings
    folded up under the
    hard wings.
Butterflies and moths, too,
    have two pairs of wings.
Their two pairs are much alike.

Many insects walk about.

Flea

Io Moth

Even some that can fly do
    a great deal of walking.

Carpenter Ant

Some insects have just one
    pair of wings.
Flies and mosquitoes do.
Silverfish do not have wings.

Dung beetles, or tumblebugs,
    often walk along pushing
    a ball of dung.

Their name tells you
    that grasshoppers hop.
Water bugs swim.

Dung Beetle

Water striders "skate" about
    on top of the water.
Many baby insects crawl.
Many insects are "turn-into"
    animals.

Giant Water Bug

The babies do not look at all
    like the grown-up insects.
A June bug is a soft white grub
    when it is first hatched.

It eats and eats
    and grows and grows.
Then it rests.

June Bug

It changes into a grown-up
    June bug.
Some insects do a great deal
    of harm.
We call them insect pests.
Clothes moths make holes
    in woolen coats and suits
    and dresses.

Clothes Moth

Silverfish spoil books.
Termites eat wood.
Sometimes they ruin houses.
Some insects eat corn or wheat.

Termite

Some eat cotton.

Corn Earworm

Some eat apples or peaches or pears.

Codling Moth

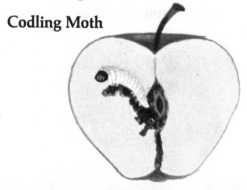

Some eat the leaves of plants.

Cabbage Butterfly

Bedbugs bite and wasps sting.
Ants and cockroaches
   sometimes get into food.

Mosquitoes and fleas and lice
   sometimes carry diseases.

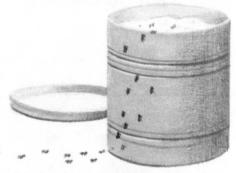

Many of the insects that harm
   us do their damage
   when they are young.

Flea

Mosquito

Body Louse

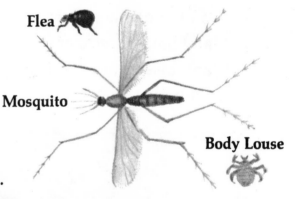

Cabbage butterflies ruin many
   cabbages.
But grown-up
   cabbage butterflies
   do not eat cabbage.
Cabbage butterflies
   do the damage
   when they are caterpillars.
Some insects help people.

Two-spotted Ladybird

Ladybird beetles, or ladybugs,
  do.
They eat plant lice,
  which harm our plants.

Dragonfly

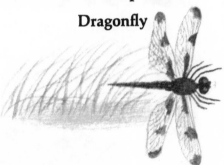

Dragonflies help us.
They eat mosquitoes.

Bees help us.
They make honey.   **Honeybee**
And they help flowers
  make seeds.
Of course, an insect does not
  mean to help or harm us.
It is just taking care
  of itself.

iron

Iron is a hard metal.
It is found in rock
  called iron ore.
Some iron ore is found
  near the surface.
Men scoop it out
  from an open pit.
Iron ore must be heated
  very hot in a furnace
  to get the iron out.
From some iron steel is made.
(Look up *steel*.)

We use a tool called an iron
  to press clothes smooth.
Irons used to be made of iron.

island

An island is land
  with water all around it.
An island may be large.

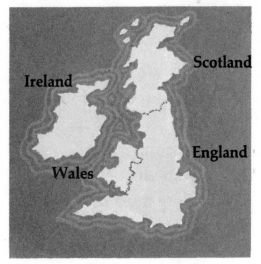

Or it may be very small.
England, Scotland and Wales
  are on one large island.

Some islands are peaks
  of undersea mountains.

Some are built up by
  tiny animals called corals.

We call them coral islands.

Some islands are made of mud
  a river has washed down
  from its banks.

ivory

Ivory comes from the tusks
  of an elephant or walrus.
It is hard and yellow-white.

It can be beautifully carved
  and polished.

jam and jelly jar

Jam and jelly are good
    to eat on bread.
To make jelly,
    boil fruit
    to get the juice.
Strain out the fruit.
Boil the juice
    with sugar.
Soon the juice thickens.
Pour it into glasses
    and put wax on top.
Jam has fruit in it
    as well as
    juice and sugar.

A cookie jar holds cookies.
A jam jar holds jam.
A jar can hold
    many kinds of things.
It is usually made of glass
    or earthenware
    and has a wide mouth.
In many lands
    women carry water
    from wells
    in water jars.

In olden days people kept
    oil or grain
    in big jars.

jellyfish

Jellyfish are
as soft as
jelly.

They are
sea animals.
They eat fish
and other sea animals.
The mouth
of a jellyfish
is on the underside
of its umbrella-like top.
A jellyfish has
streamers it uses
to get food into its mouth.

jet plane

Jet planes have jet engines.
A jet engine sends hot gas
pouring out the back
in a "jet."
The hot gas inside the engine
pushes the plane ahead.

Some jet planes are small.
They hold just one man.
Some jet planes are large.

They carry 100 people or more.
They fly very fast.
Jet engines make a great roar.
They make jet trails
in the sky.
(Look up *aircraft*.)

J

jewelry

We wear jewelry
   for decoration.
Rings for our fingers
   are jewelry.
So are bracelets for our arms.
Pretty pins are jewelry.
So are necklaces and beads.
So are earrings for our ears
   and clips for neckties.

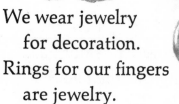

Some jewelry
   is made of silver or gold.
Some jewelry has jewels in it.
Jewels are pretty, bright stones.
Diamonds are jewels.
So are red rubies
   and green emeralds.
Jewels come in many colors.

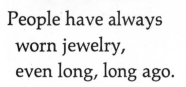

People have always
   worn jewelry,
   even long, long ago.

In some countries people wear
   most of their riches
   in jewelry.

juggler

A juggler does tricks.
He can keep balls or plates
　spinning in the air.
He is quick and clever.

jungle

A jungle is a thick forest.
(Look up *forest*.)
It is hot and wet.
The trees grow close together.
Some of the trees have
　tall, tall trunks.
These trees are tall enough
　to get lots of sunlight.
They branch out above
　the shorter trees.
In a jungle
　some trees start growing
　in the tops of other trees.
They send long roots
　to the ground.

Many plants besides trees
　grow in a jungle.
There are low ferns and bushes.
They get little sunlight.
There are vines that climb up
　the trunks of trees
　into the sunlight.
And some of the small
　plants of a jungle
　perch on the
　branches of trees.
Many kinds of orchids
　are jungle perchers.

J

Many animals
   live in the jungle, too.
In the rivers
   there are fish
   and alligators and crocodiles.
On the ground
   there are panthers
   and anteaters
   and many other animals.

In the trees
   there are monkeys
   and snakes.
There are parrots
   and other beautiful birds.
All over the jungle
   there are many insects.
A jungle is full
   of living things.

kangaroo

A mother kangaroo
  has a pouch.
Her babies grow up in it.
They get some fine rides.
For a kangaroo can leap
  the length of a room
  in one leap.
Kangaroos live in Australia.
They hunt for grass
  and other plants to eat.

king

A king rules his country.
It is called a kingdom.
A king's wife is a queen.
The king's sons are princes.
His daughters are princesses.
In olden days there were
  many kings and kingdoms.
Most kings
  were born to be kings.
Today there are not many kings.
They do not have
  very much power.
There are not many kingdoms.
There are more republics.
The people choose their leaders
  in a republic.
But in fairy tales
  there are many kings
  and queens,
  handsome princes
  and beautiful princesses.

kitchen

Food is cooked in a kitchen.
You need heat for cooking.
(Look up *cooking*
    and *food*.)
The kitchen may have
    an electric stove.

It may have a stove that burns
    gas, wood, coal or kerosene.
Or the food may be cooked
    over a pot
    that burns charcoal.

You need water in a kitchen.
The water may come
    from pipes leading to a sink.
The water may come
    from a pump.
Or you may have to put
    a bucket down a well
    and carry the water
    into the kitchen.
To keep food cold and fresh
    you may have a freezer
    and a refrigerator.
Your kitchen may have
    cupboards full of jars
    and cans and packages.
You need bowls and pots
    and pans in a kitchen.
You need knives and forks
    and spoons.
You may have a big kitchen
    or a small kitchen.
The kitchen
    is an important place.

K

kite

A kite flies.
It flies on a breeze.
A kite must be very light.
Most kites are made of paper.
A flat kite needs a tail.
The tail holds one end down.
Then the breeze can push
   the kite up
   and make it fly.
A box kite does not need a tail.
Some kites are big and beautiful.
The most beautiful kites
   are those of China and Japan.

Some kites are so big
   a boy or girl
   or a grown man
   can ride one
   up into the air.

knife

A knife cuts.
A knife has a sharp blade.

It has a handle to hold it by.

Cavemen long, long ago
   made blades
   of stone or bone.
Today most knife blades
   are made of steel.
(Look up *steel*.)
The knives we set
   our tables with
   are silver or stainless steel.
They match
   the forks and spoons.

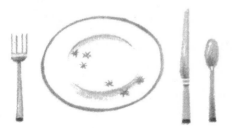

knitting

Women knit sweaters.
They use knitting needles.
They pull loops of yarn
   into other loops
   with the needles.
Women may knit socks
   and caps.

They may knit mittens, too,
   and many other things.

Knitted things are warm
   and snug.
Now many
   knitted things
   are made by machine.

K

knot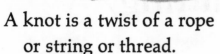

A knot is a twist of a rope
 or string or thread.
A knot will not come undone
 easily.
We learn to tie bowknots
 in shoelaces.

The knot keeps the laces snug.
Our mothers make a knot
 in the end of a thread
 when they start to sew.

A cowboy makes a big loop
 in his rope lariat.
Then he makes a slipknot.
The loop tightens
 when he pulls
 on the end of the rope.
The lariat can stop
 a running cow.

A sailor learns to make
 many knots.

So do scouts and campers.
Here are a few knots to try.

koala

A koala looks
 like a fuzzy little bear.
But it is more like a kangaroo.
Mother koala carries her baby
 in a pouch like a kangaroo.
Later the baby rides piggyback.
Koalas live in Australia.
They sleep all day
 high up in a gum tree.

laboratory

A laboratory is a room
   where scientists work.
Scientists do different
   kinds of work.

Some study rocks.
Some study plants.

Some study animals.
Some study stars.
There are many sciences.
(Look up *science*.)

Scientists have different kinds
   of laboratories.
In their laboratories
   they carry on experiments.
They have a great deal
   of laboratory equipment
   to work with.
Most laboratories have outlets
   for electricity
   and sinks for running water.
Most of them have long tables.
They have stools
   for the scientists to sit on.
On top of the tables
   are machines
   and tools and containers.
Scientists often heat things.
They may use gas burners
   called Bunsen burners.

lace

Lace is pretty.
It is made of thread.
So is cloth.
But lace is more open
    than cloth.
Brides like to have veils
    made of lace
    or trimmed with lace.

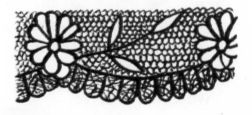

Scientists sometimes
    heat things in glass
    so they can see what happens.
They use special glass
    that does not break
    when it gets hot.
They have glass containers
    of different kinds—
    flasks and bottles
    and beakers
    and test tubes.
Scientists measure things.
They may have scales
    or calipers
    or other tools for measuring.
A scientist may have helpers
    in his laboratory.
They are called
    laboratory assistants.

Most lace today
    is made by machine.
But the finest lace
    is still made by hand.
Tatting is a handmade lace.
The thread is wound on
    a shuttle, or bobbin.
The shuttle is moved swiftly
    in and out among threads
    in the lacemaker's fingers.

L

Some fine lace
is made
by twisting threads around
pins stuck in a pillow.
The pins mark the pattern.
Making beautiful lace
is hard work for the eyes.

In olden days gentlemen
as well as ladies
wore lots of lace.

lady

A lady is a woman
who is pleasant
and thoughtful
and nice to be with.
Any little girl
can grow up to be
a lady.

lake

A lake is water
with land all around it.
A very small lake
may be called a pond.
A very large lake
may be called a sea.
Most lakes get their water
from rains
and melting snows.
Streams bring the water
to the lake.
Most lakes have rivers
running out of them.
The rivers carry lake water
to the oceans far away.

Some lakes have big cities
on their shores.

Some lakes are high
in the mountains.

Some lakes are low
in the desert.

Their water may be salty.

Big ships cross these lakes
to the cities.
Some lakes are better
for small boats—rowboats
or canoes.
Many people spend vacations
at cottages on lakes.
They swim and boat and fish
and have a happy time.

lamp

A lamp
    gives light.
Most lamps
    in our homes
    today are
    electric lamps.

An electric lamp
    must have wires
    to bring electricity.

It must have
    a bulb or tube
    to give out light.

They may be
    on walls or ceilings.
Some lamps
    stand on tables.
We call them table lamps.
Some stand on the floor.
We call them floor lamps.
We can move these lamps about.

Before the days of electricity,
    lamps burned gas
    or kerosene or other oil.
The oil traveled up a wick.
Some had glass chimneys.
Some had pretty shades as well.
Very early oil lamps
    were just little bowls
    that held the oil and wick.

lantern

A lantern
  is a light in a case.
We may use a lantern
  to see by out-of-doors.
The case protects the light.
Long ago people
  carried torches
  of burning sticks or reeds
  to light their way at night.
But rain or wind
  could put out a torch.
So they began to put
  a covering around the flame.
Most of our lanterns
  have covers of glass.
Some lanterns
  have covers
  of paper.
Japanese lanterns do.
They are very pretty.
Some Japanese lanterns
  have fireflies inside
  to give the light.

In olden days
  oil lanterns
  lighted some
  city streets.

Gas lamps took their place.
A lamplighter had to light
  each lamp when evening came.

Now most street lights
  are electric.
So are automobile headlights
  and many hand lanterns.
A lantern tower
  beside the sea
  is called a lighthouse.
A lantern floating on the sea
  is called a light buoy.
Lighthouses and light buoys
  warn sailors of rocks.

L

laundry

We wash our clothes,
  linens and towels
    to make them clean.
We call these things laundry
  when we wash them.
We say we launder them.
We may send our clothes
  to a big laundry.

A laundryman picks them up.
Or our mother may
  wash them herself
  in a washing machine.
She puts the clothes in.
She adds soap powder.
She closes the door.
She turns on the machine.
Water runs in.
The clothes swish around.
Soon they are clean.
Maybe our mother
  uses a drying machine, too.
She puts in the wet clothes.

She turns on the machine.
Soon they are dry.
In most lands,
  mothers do not have
  machines like ours.

They may use washtubs.
They may rub clothes
  on washboards
  to get the dirt out.
They hang the clothes out
  to dry on clotheslines,
  or they spread them out
  in the sun.

In some lands, all the women
  of the village
  do their laundry together.
They take their clothes
  to the village fountain.
They have a good visit
  while they wash.
Or they may go to a river
  or a lake.
They may wash their clothes
  on the stones
  along the bank or shore.
They spread out their clothes
  in the sun to dry.

In some places,
  washermen wash clothes
  in bundles.
They lift the wet bundles
  and slam them down on rocks
  time after time
  to loosen the dirt.
They press the clothes smooth
  with flatirons
  filled with hot coals.
In every land,
  people like to have
  nice, clean clothes
  to wear.

L

lead pencil

A lead pencil is to write
and draw with.
Lead is a heavy gray metal.
But really there is no lead
in a pencil.
The black is graphite.
It is mixed with clay,
squeezed out thin
and baked.

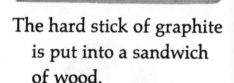

The hard stick of graphite
is put into a sandwich
of wood.
The two pieces of wood
are stuck together.
The pencil is painted.
Sometimes an eraser
is added at one end.

If you make a mistake,
you can rub it out
with the eraser.

leaf

In the summer most leaves
are green.

Coleus

Caladium

But there are some red leaves
and yellow leaves
and spotted leaves.

Birch

Maple

In the fall many leaves
change color.
Leaves are not all
the same size.

White Oak

Palm

Palm leaves are very big.

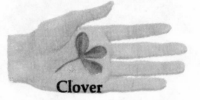

Clover

Clover leaves are little.

Leaves are not all
    the same shape.

Water Lily

Olive

Blackjack Oak

Redbud

Some are round.
Some are heart-shaped.
Some are long and narrow.

A leaf always has veins in it.
Veins are tiny pipes
    for carrying water and food.
The veins in a leaf
    make a pattern.
They do not all
    make the same pattern.
A leaf is a tiny factory.
It makes food for the plant
    it grows on.
Sugar is one of the foods
    a leaf makes.
It uses water and a part
    of the air to make sugar.
A factory has to have energy
    to make it run.
A leaf factory gets its energy
    from sunshine.

Pine

Many evergreen trees have
    leaves so long and narrow
    that they are called needles.
Some leaves are shaped
    like mittens.

Sassafras

Some leaves are made up
    of little leaflets.

Staghorn Sumac

This is just one leaf
    of a sumac bush.

Osage Orange   **Elm**

Some leaves have smooth edges.
Some have edges like a saw.

Locust

L

leather

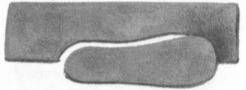

Leather is made
  from animal skin.
The skin or hide of cows,
  goats and pigs
  makes good leather.

So does the skin of alligators
  and crocodiles and of some
  snakes and lizards.

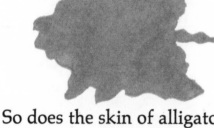

The skin must be cleaned
  and scraped.
Then it is tanned.
It may be soaked
  in a mixture made
  from the bark
  of certain trees.
It may be tanned
  in other ways.
After the tanning,
  the skin is treated with oil.

Leather may be thick and stiff.
Or it may be thin and soft.

Shoe soles are made
  from thick, stiff leather.

So are some suitcases.

Gloves and ladies' shoes are
  made from soft, thin leather.
Some leather is rubbed
  to look like soft cloth.
It is called suede.
Some leather is polished
  to shine.
Good leather lasts a long time.

lens

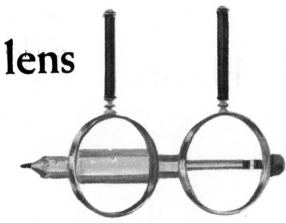

A lens is usually
   made of glass.
It has a special shape.
When we look at things
   through a lens,
   they look bigger or smaller.
A lens thick in the middle
   makes things look bigger.
We say it magnifies.
A lens thin in the middle
   makes things look smaller.
Our eyes have lenses inside
   to help us see well.
Of course, these lenses
   are not glass.

Telescopes have lenses.
A telescope helps us see
   the moon and stars better.

Eyeglasses have lenses.
They make people see better.
Cameras have lenses.

Microscopes have lenses.
A microscope helps us see
   tiny things better.
Scientists use lenses
   in many ways.
Some use microscopes.
Some use telescopes.
Some use other instruments
   with lenses in them.
Scientists learn many things
   by using lenses.

letter

The alphabet is made up
of letters.
(Look up *alphabet*.)
Every word in this book
is made up of letters.
There is another kind of letter.
A letter brings us news
from someone.
Or we may
write a letter
to tell someone how we are,
to say, "Thank you,"
or to send our love.
We fold the letter
and put it
in an envelope.
We write on the envelope
the name of the person
the letter is for.
We write where he lives.
And we mail the letter.
(Look up *mail* to see
what happens then.)

library

A library is a place for books.
Some homes have a book room
called a library.

You may have a library corner
in your own room.
There have been libraries
as long as there have been books.
(Look up *book*.)

182

Some libraries are on wheels.
They are called bookmobiles.
If you live in the country,
    a bookmobile may come.
You can borrow books.
You can return those
    you have read.

Most towns have a library.
You get a library card.
It has your name on it.
Then you can borrow books
    from the library.
There is a librarian
    at the desk.
The librarian will help you
    choose a book if you wish.
There are lots and lots of books
    on shelves.
There are tables with chairs
    just the right size
    if you want to sit and read.
This is fun.
A library is a friendly place
    to go to.

Some libraries are huge.
You can read books all your life.
There will always be more
    for you to read!

light

We need light to see by.
Daylight is light
   we get from the sun.
The sun is very bright.
Its light falls on a flower.
The light bounces
   from the flower to our eyes.
We see the flower.
Sunlight falls on a friend's face.
The light bounces from the face
   to our eyes.

We see our friend.

In shadows
   where sunlight is not strong
   we do not see so well.

At night
   the sun is not shining
   on our part of the earth.
(Look up *day* and *night*.)
But it may be shining
   on the moon up in the sky.
The sunlight bounces
   from the moon to our eyes.

We see the moon.
Stars are like our sun.
They give bright light, too.
But stars are very far away.
We cannot see to do things
   by their light.
The sun and stars give light
   because they are hot—
   hotter than fire.
Fire gives light, too.

Candlelight is firelight.

Electric light bulbs give light
because wires inside them
get white-hot.

When the light falls
    on an open book at night,
    light bounces to our eyes.
And we can see to read.
Wherever there is light
    to light up the dark,
    we can see.

lighthouse

A lighthouse is a tower
    that has a big light
    at the top.
It warns ships
    of rocks and sandbars.
A lighthouse keeper
    keeps the light burning.
He may sound a foghorn, too.
When it is hard
    to see the light
    through the fog or storm,
    sailors will hear
    the deep voice
    of the foghorn.
They will know that rocks
    or shallows are near.
(Look up *fog*
    and *lantern*.)

L

linen

Linen is a kind of cloth
made from flax plants.
(Look up *cloth*.)
To make linen
you cut the flax stems.
You soak the stems in water.
Stringy fibers in the stems
come loose.
You comb these fibers straight.
You stretch them out.
While they are wet,
you spin them into thread.
This is linen thread.
You can weave it into cloth.

Heavy linen cloth makes sails
for sailboats.
It is called sailcloth.
Fine linen makes handkerchiefs
and tablecloths and napkins.
Linen makes pretty tea towels
and suits and dresses, too.

linoleum

Linoleum covers floors.
It is easy to clean.
It cuts down noise.

Linoleum is good for rooms
where children play.
It is good for kitchens, too.

lion

The lion
is a big
wild animal.
It is
a
cousin
of the cat.
(Look up *cat*.)

The lion is called
the king of beasts.
It has a loud roar.
The father lion
has a mane of heavy hair
on his neck and head.
The mother lion
is called a lioness.
She has no mane.
The mother lion
takes care of the babies.
They are called cubs.
You can see lions
in almost any circus or zoo.
Most lions come from Africa.

lizard

Lizards are reptiles.
They are related
to alligators, crocodiles,
turtles and snakes.

Most lizards live
where it is warm
the year around.

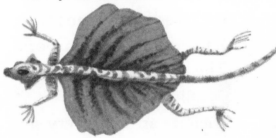

Lizards can run fast.
The flying dragon can almost fly.
Some lizards are rather large.
But all lizards of today
are tiny compared with
their giant dinosaur cousins
of long ago.

(Look up *dinosaur* and *reptiles*.)

187

llama

lobster

The llama is a mountain animal.
It lives in the high Andes
in South America.
The llama has been tamed.
We say it is a domestic animal.
It carries heavy loads.
Its wool makes good cloth.
The llama has a wild cousin
called the vicuña.
Vicuñas are very, very shy.
Their wool is fine and soft.
It makes soft, warm cloth
that is light and beautiful.

A lobster is a sea animal.
It has a hard covering.
As it grows,
a lobster sheds its hard coat
and grows a bigger one.
Lobster meat is good to eat.
Lobster fishermen put down
lobster pots to catch lobsters.
They put dead fish in them.
Lobsters eat dead fish.
They walk into the pots.
Then they cannot walk out again.
They are trapped.

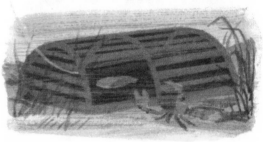

lock

A lock closes a door or box
   so it cannot be opened easily.
Most locks need a key
   to open them.

locomotive

Older kinds
   of electric locomotives
   get their electricity
   from distant power plants.

The electricity may come
   to these locomotives
   through wires overhead,
   or through a third rail
   running along the track.
(Look up *railroad*.)

(Look up *railroad*.)

A locomotive is an engine
   that runs a train.
The most modern locomotives
   are Diesel-electrics.
Diesel engines burn oil
   to make electricity.
The electricity drives
   the locomotive.

The earliest locomotives
   had steam engines.
They were steam locomotives.
They had a firebox.
The fire boiled water.
The water boiled into steam.
The steam pushed parts
   that turned the wheels.

L

Steam locomotives
   used a lot of water.
Big water tanks stood
   beside the tracks
   to fill the boilers
   of the locomotives.

Early steam locomotives
   were small.

Later ones were big
   and powerful.
They used a great deal of coal.
A coal car came
   behind the locomotive.
So it was easy to shovel
   more coal into the firebox.

A steam locomotive had a bell.
The engineer could ring it.
A steam locomotive
   had a whistle, too.
When the engineer pulled a cord,
   the whistle blew.
What a wonderful sound!

lumbering

Lumber is wood
   cut into boards and planks.
Lumber is used for building.
(Look up *furniture*
   and *house*.)
Trees are cut in the forest
   by men called lumberjacks.
The men live in lumber camps.
They sleep on bunks
   in a bunkhouse.
They eat in the cookhouse.
Some cut branches
   from tall trees.
Some saw through the trunks
   of trees
   to make them fall.

When a tree falls,
   it is sawed into logs.
The logs are hauled away
   on a truck.
Or a lumberjack with a tractor
   takes the logs
   to a little narrow railroad
   or to a river.
He may slide them down a slide
   into the river.
The logs float
   down the river to the sawmill.

At the sawmill,
   the logs are split by saws.
They are cut into neat pieces
   of lumber.
Each one is a special size.
The lumber is stacked up
   so that air can reach it.
The wood dries out.
It is ready to use.

Trucks and trains carry it away
   to towns and cities.
Every city and town
   has a lumberyard.
The lumberyard has stacks
   of boards and planks
   of many sizes.
It has lumber
   from different kinds of trees.
There you can buy
   all the wood you need
   to build a house.

machine

Machines help us do work.
With machines we can do work
    faster and more easily
    than without them.
A typewriter
    is a writing machine.
A person can write a letter
    faster by typewriter
    than by hand.

With a washing machine,
    a mother can do
    her washing
    faster than by hand.
With a vacuum cleaner
    a mother can do
    her cleaning
    more easily
    than with a broom.

A machine has parts that move.
Some kind of power
    has to make them move.
Many machines use man power.
Most typewriters do.
Other machines
    are run by electricity.
Vacuum cleaners
    and washing machines are.
Many machines are run
    by heat engines.
Cars and airplanes are.
There are machines
    that do arithmetic
    quickly and easily.
Some are very big.
They are called electric brains.

Sometimes we use machines
    instead of walking.

Machines help us build houses
and other buildings.

Machines help us build roads.

It used to take hundreds of people
to build roads and buildings
that now a few people
with big machines can build.

Machines lift heavy loads for us.

Machines carry for us.

Machines plant for us.
Machines weed the fields.

Machines harvest the crops.

Machines spin our thread
and weave our cloth
and sew our clothes.
All this work people used to do
by hand.

Machines make our paper.
Others print our books.

magnet

A magnet attracts things
  made of iron or steel.
"Attracts" means "pulls."
Put some steel pins on a table.
Hold a magnet close to them.
The pins will jump up
  and touch the magnet.
It may be hard to get them off.
A magnet has a south pole
  and a north pole.
It pulls hardest at its poles.
The earth is a giant magnet.
Its magnetic poles are
  near the North Pole
  and the South Pole.
A compass tells directions
  because its needle is a magnet
  that points to the north pole
  of the earth magnet.
Magnets called electromagnets
  work only when electricity
  is going through them.
Turn off the electric current.
They lose their magnetism.
Many machines have
  electromagnets in them.

Machines cut our wood
  and smooth and shape it.
Machines shape many
  of the metal things we use.
Machines pump our water.

Machines milk our cows
  and bottle the milk.
We can have many more things
  and can live more comfortably,
  because we have machines
  to help us with our work.

mail

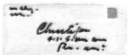

The letters, paper and packages
that come to us
from the post office are mail.
The letters, papers and packages
we take to the post office
or drop in the mailbox
are mail, too.

Suppose you want to send
a letter to a friend.
You put the letter in an envelope.
On the envelope
you write his name
and address.
You put a stamp on
to pay for all the work
the mailmen do.
Suppose you take your letter
to the post office.

Mailmen there sort the mail.
Your letter may be going
out of town.

If it is, it is put
into a big mail sack.
It is put on a truck or train
or airplane.

Let's say your letter
goes by train.

On the train
the sack with your letter in it
may be opened in a mail car.
The mail car is like a post office.
Your letter is sorted.
It is put with the other mail
going to the same town.
At the right town,
off it goes.
It goes to the post office.

And that very day
the postman, or mailman
may drop it
into your friend's mailbox.

M

map

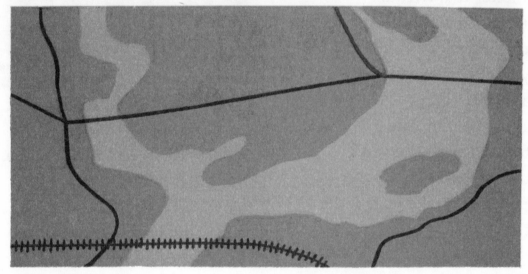

A map can show you
how to get to where
you want to go.
A map is a little like
a picture of a town
or country
taken from high up
in the air.
A map is clearer than a picture.

It picks out
the important things
to show
roads, _____ _____
railroads, +++++++++++++
rivers, ∼∼∼∼∼∼∼
lakes, ⬯
mountains ⬭
and cities. ● ○ ◎

Some maps can even tell you
   how good a road is,
   how deep a lake is,
   how high a mountain is,
   and how large a city is.

See if you can find
   on the map below
   a road, a river, a lake,
   a railroad, a mountain
   and a city.

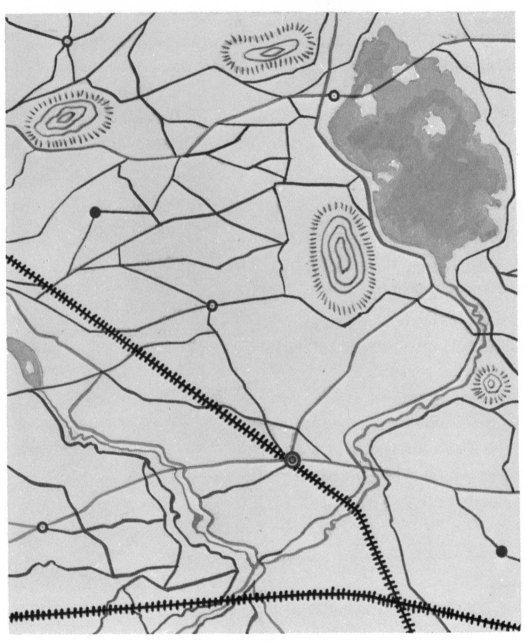

M

marble

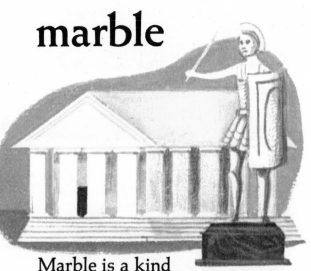

Marble is a kind
of stone or rock.
It comes in pretty colors.
It often has pretty patterns
in it.
Marble can be carved.
It can be polished, too.
Marble is often used
in fine big buildings
and for statues.
All marble was once limestone—
a kind of rock made
at the bottom of a sea.
In time, deep down in the earth,
the limestone was heated and
pressed till it became marble.
(Look up *rock*.)

marbles

Marbles is a game.
You play it with little balls.

They are called marbles.
You put some of them in a ring.
You try to shoot them
out of the ring
with other marbles,
often slightly bigger.
Marbles may be made of clay.
They may be made of
different kinds
of stones.

The ones made of agate
are called "aggies."
But most marbles today
are made of glass.
Marbles can be pretty.
Marbles is a good game.

market

A market is where things are
   sold.
In warm countries,
   many things are sold
   out-of-doors.
The picture shows
   an outdoor market.
The market place like this
   is often in the center of town.
People like to come to market.
They come in from the country.
They bring foods to sell.
They bring things
   they have made.
They see their friends.
They have a good time
   on market day.

We may buy our food
   and many other things
   in big, bright markets
   called supermarkets.
We take a cart.
We push it along.
We fill it up
   with things we need or want.
We can even buy books
   in a supermarket.

M

mask

A mask hides your face.
It makes you look different.
You may wear a mask
   or a half mask
   on Halloween.
You may wear a mask to a party.
A party where you wear a mask
   and dress as someone else
   is called a masquerade.
In olden times
   people used to wear masks
   when they acted in plays.
The mask showed
   if the person in the play
   was happy or sad.

In some lands
   people still wear masks
   when they dance
   or act on the stage.

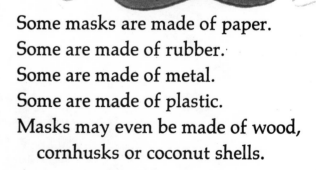

Some masks are made of paper.
Some are made of rubber.
Some are made of metal.
Some are made of plastic.
Masks may even be made of wood,
   cornhusks or coconut shells.

meat

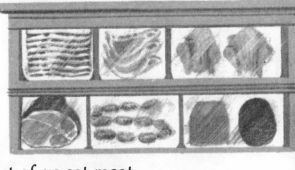

Most of us eat meat.
We may eat the meat of cattle.
Beef and veal come from cattle.
We may eat the meat of pigs.
Bacon and ham and pork
   come from pigs.
We may eat the meat of sheep.
Lamb or mutton come from sheep.
We may eat the meat
   of chickens, ducks,
   geese or turkeys.
Meat is good for us.
It tastes good, too.
Nearly everyone
   has a favorite kind.
Some like steak best.
Some like chicken.
Some like lamb chops
   or pork chops.
Some like ham.
You can have many people
   for dinner with a large ham.

Some like turkey,
   especially for Thanksgiving.

Some like their meat ground up.

Hamburger is ground beef.
Sausage is ground pork.
Frankfurters are beef and pork
   ground up together.
Some people do not eat meat.
They are called vegetarians.

medicine

Medicine helps make us well
  if we are sick.
Medicine helps keep us well
  if we are healthy.
Our doctor knows about
  the medicines we need.
He may say,
  "Fresh air and good food and
  lots of sleep and exercise
  are the best medicines."
He means that they will
  help keep us well.
He may give us shots
  to keep us from getting
  certain diseases.
Or he may give us medicine
  to swallow to make us well.

mermaid

A mermaid is a make-believe
  person.
She is half girl, half fish.
She lives in a palace
  at the bottom of the sea.
Sometimes she comes up
  to sit on the rocks and sing.

Stories tell us that sailors
  may fall in love with
  a mermaid and her song.

metal

Most metals are hard.
They can be pounded
    into different shapes.
They can be hammered flat
    or drawn out
    in thin threads called wire.
But one metal is a liquid.
It is mercury, or quicksilver.
You may have seen it
    in a thermometer.
Other metals are liquid
    when they are very hot.

We call them molten metals.
Gold and silver are metals.
(Look up *gold*
    and *silver*.)
Iron is a metal.
(Look up *iron*.)

Most metal is found
    in rock called ore.
Ore must be heated
    to get the metal
    out of the rock.
When the metal is melted
    it can be poured into a form
    called a mold.
Much of the metal we use
    is a mixture of metals.
Steel and brass are mixtures.
So are pewter and bronze.
We have many things
    made of metal—

M

aluminum pots and pans,
copper and steel pots,

steel knives and tableware.
We have silver and pewter,
    brass and copper bowls
    and candlesticks.
We use cans and coins
    of metal, too.
We use metals every day.

microscope

Double Eyepiece

Lenses

Slide

Platform

Electric Light

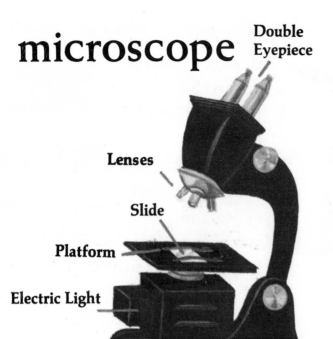

A microscope lets us see
   very tiny things.
We put a sample
   of what we want to study
   on a piece of glass
   called a slide.
We cover it with a piece
   of very thin glass.
We put the slide on the platform.
We look through the eyepiece.
Lenses in the microscope
   make the sample on the slide
   look large and clear.
(Look up *lens*.)
We learn many things
   by using microscopes.

milk

Milk is the food
   many mammal mothers
   have for their babies.

Often cows give more milk
   than their babies need.
So there is some left
   for people to drink.
(Look up *cattle*
   and *dairy farms*.)
In some cold lands
   people drink reindeer's milk.

In some hot deserts
  people drink camel's milk.

In some mountains
  people drink goat's milk.

In some low, hot lands
  people drink the milk
  of the water buffalo.

There are other animals, too,
  which give milk
  that people drink.
Llamas, yaks and sheep
  are three of them.

We make many foods from milk.
Butter and cheese,
  whipped cream
  and ice cream
  are made from it.
(Look up *cheese*
  and *ice cream*.)
We all need milk
  and milk foods every day.

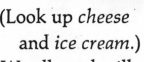

Milky Way

On a clear night,
  we sometimes see a pale band
  of light across the sky.
It is the Milky Way.
The Milky Way is made up
  of billions of stars.
There are so many stars
  and they are so far away
  that we cannot see them
  as separate stars.
We see only the band of light
  across the sky.
(Look up *sky*.)

minerals

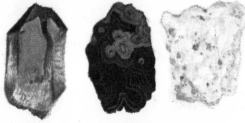

Minerals are hard.
They make up rock.
Most rocks are made
    of two or three minerals.
(Look up *rock*.)
Often minerals are in
    crystals.
A crystal has a regular shape.
Here are some crystal shapes.

In rock, the crystals
    may be crowded together.
They may not be perfect.
Many people like
    to go hiking to collect
    pretty samples of minerals.
These people sometimes are
    called "rock hounds."

Most of our minerals
    are under the ground.
We dig mines to get them out.
(Look up *coal, iron,*
    and *salt*
    for different kinds
    of mines.)

Water may have minerals
    dissolved in it.
In some caves
    underground water falls,
    drop by drop,
    down from the roof.
The minerals from the water
    collect on the roof
    or the floor of the cave.
They form stone "icicles."

The soil has minerals in it.
Soil is made mostly
    of tiny bits of rock.
Rock is made of minerals.
Therefore soil has minerals.
Some of the minerals
    in the soil
    dissolve in water.
The water carries them
    into plants growing
    in the soil.
By eating some of the plants
    and by drinking the milk
    and eating the meat
    of animals that eat plants,
    we get minerals we need.
The minerals help keep us well.
They make us grow strong
    and have good bones.
We need to drink milk
    and eat meat and fruit,
    cereals and vegetables,
    to get the minerals we need.

mirror

You can see yourself
    in a mirror.

A mirror bounces back
    the light that strikes it.
A mirror must be very smooth.
Usually smooth glass is used.
Most glass mirrors have
    a silver backing.

A pool of water may be a mirror.
The smooth surface of the water
    bounces light back.
So you see in the pool
    whatever is on its banks.
Old-time mirrors were made
    of smooth, polished metal.
Mirrors are used
    in kaleidoscopes
    and periscopes
    and microscopes
    and telescopes.

money

We pay for things with money.
We use metal coins and
    paper bills for money.
Pennies, nickels, dimes,
    quarters, half dollars
    and dollars are names
    for our money.
People in other lands
    have different names
    for their money.
They may speak
    of shillings and pounds,
    of francs or marks,
    of liras or rupees.
Their money may not look
    much like ours,
    but most of it
    is made of metal or paper.

Many other things have been used
    as money.

Here are some of them:

seashells,

oxen or cattle,

coconuts,

rings of stone,

sacks of grain,

horses,

arrowheads,

camels,

furs,

blankets or cloth,

dried fish,

gold dust.

All these have been used
in one place or another.
(Look up *wampum*.)
But coins or bills are handier.
So most people use them now.

monkey

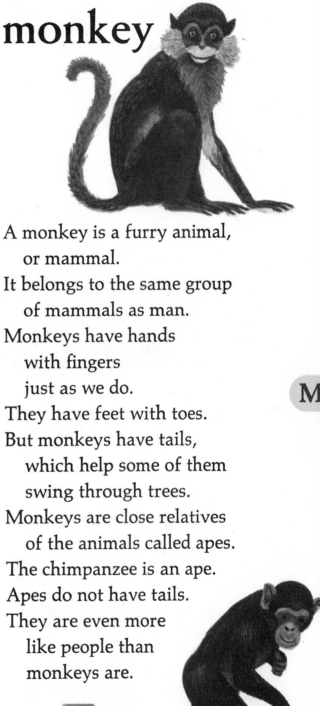

A monkey is a furry animal,
or mammal.
It belongs to the same group
of mammals as man.
Monkeys have hands
with fingers
just as we do.
They have feet with toes.
But monkeys have tails,
which help some of them
swing through trees.
Monkeys are close relatives
of the animals called apes.
The chimpanzee is an ape.
Apes do not have tails.
They are even more
like people than
monkeys are.

M

moon

We see the moon
in the sky at night,
and sometimes
in the daytime, too.
The moon does not shine
by its own light.
We see it only when sunlight
bounces to us from the moon.
(Look up *light*.)

Sometimes the moon looks
big and round.
We call it a full moon.
The sun is shining then
on all of the side of the moon
turned toward us.

So we see a big bright circle.
Usually the sun is shining
on only part of the side
of the moon toward us.
Then we see only
part of a circle.
The shape of the moon seems
to change from day to day.
The moon is really
a huge ball of rock
that travels around the earth.
The moon has high mountains
just as the earth has.
But it has no water or air.
It has no plants or animals.
Some day men will visit
the moon.
They will find the days long
and terribly hot.
The long nights will be
terribly cold.

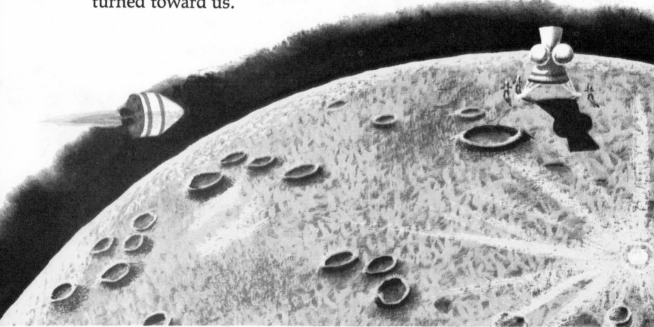

moss

Moss is a kind of tiny plant
  that grows
  in damp, shady spots.
Many, many tiny moss plants
  grow very close together.
They often make
  a soft green carpet
  on wet ground.
They grow on stones
  and tree trunks, too.
Mosses are very simple.
They have no real roots
  or stems or leaves.
They have no flowers.
But they have stalks like stems
  and greenery like leaves.
And they have tiny spores
  instead of seeds.

M

Mother Goose

Everyone knows Little Miss Muffet,
  Little Boy Blue,
  Little Jack Horner
  and Mistress Mary Quite Contrary.
They are all friends
  from rhymes once told,
  it is said,
  by a lady named Mother Goose.

mountain

A mountain is very high.
It is made of rock.
It may be so high
   that the snow on the top
   never melts.
It may have sharp peaks.
Young mountains
   have sharp peaks.
But rain and ice and wind
   all work together to change
   the shape of mountains.
Pieces break off.
The mountains grow
   rounder.

Old mountains have had
   their sharp peaks
   worn down.
Trees may cover their tops.
Some mountains are built up
   by hot melted rock
   bubbling up from
   deep inside the earth.
They are called volcanoes.

moving pictures

Most of us like to watch
   moving pictures.
We call them "movies."
Some people have
   moving-picture cameras.
(Look up *camera*.)

We can see their "movies"
   at home.
We may even see ourselves
   in them.

Some movies
   we see on television.
Some movies we see in theaters.
Some movies we see in school.
Moving pictures are fun to see.
And we can learn from them.

mushroom

A mushroom is a plant.
It grows mostly underground.
It does not have flowers.
Like moss and ferns,
   a mushroom has spores
   instead of seeds.
The mushroom in the picture
   is a meadow mushroom.
When an underground
   meadow mushroom plant
   is ready to send out spores,
   it shoots up a "button"
   through the soil.
The "button" spreads out
   like an umbrella.
From underneath the "umbrella"
   ripe spores puff out like dust.
Many mushroms are good to eat.
But some make us very sick.
We should never
   eat wild mushrooms
   we do not know are safe.

music

Music is made up
   of sounds that are pleasant
   to hear.
We make music
   with our voices
   when we sing.
If we sing different notes
   that sound well together,
   we call it harmony.
We make music
   with musical instruments.
We can beat on drums.
(Look up *drum*.)

We can toot on horns.

We can blow on piccolos
   and flutes.

We can pluck violin
   and cello strings
   or stroke them with a bow.

With all these instruments
   we can have an orchestra.
(Look up *orchestra*.)

nail

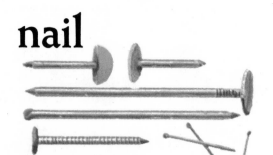

We nail wood together.
A nail is slim and straight.
It is usually made of metal.
It has a point at one end
    to go into the wood.
It has a flat head
    at the other end.

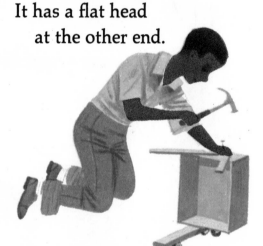

We can drive in a nail
    by pounding on its head
    with a hammer.
If we want to pull
    a nail out,
    we may use the nail puller
    on the hammer.

Nails are used
    in building houses.
Carpenters use nails.

Nails are used
    in making furniture.
A cabinetmaker uses nails.

A small nail is called
    a tack
    or a brad.
Some tacks you can push in
    with your thumb.
They are called thumbtacks.
A very large nail
    is called a spike.
A sort of nail made of wood
    is called a peg.
A peg needs a hole
    it can fit into.
You cannot fit a square peg
    into a round hole.

navy

A navy is made up of ships,
   planes and men.
It works mainly at sea.
A navy helps to keep
   its country safe.
Its ships and planes
   are armed with weapons.
Navy men are called sailors
   or seamen.
Some navy men work on shore.
They work at naval bases.

narwhal

A narwhal is a small whale.
(Look up *whale*.)
It lives in cold northern seas.
The father narwhal
   has a long tusk.
It pokes out in front of him.

N

net

A net is made
    of loosely woven threads.
It has open spaces in it.
Some nets have big spaces.
Some nets have small spaces.
A tennis net is for
    tennis balls to be hit over.

A fish net catches fish.
They cannot swim out of it.
(Look up *fishermen*.)
A mosquito net
    keeps mosquitoes away
    from your bed at night.
They cannot fly through it.
With a butterfly net
    you can catch butterflies.

If a net is made of fine thread
    and has small holes,
    we say it has a fine mesh.
Mosquito nets have a fine mesh.
If a net is made of thick thread
    and has big holes,
    we say it has a coarse mesh.
A tennis net has a coarse mesh.

news

News of the day
    tells us what is happening
    all over the world.
We hear newscasts on the radio.
We see them on television.
We read news in newspapers.
Soon what is happening
    will be history.
But today it is new.
It makes today's news.

newspaper

A newspaper comes out
   every day or every week.
It has news.
It has pictures.
It tells us what many people
   think.
It has advertisements
   to show us
   what we can buy.

Newspapermen work hard
   to put out a newspaper.
Some are reporters.
They go around
   talking to people.
They look for news.

Editors in the newspaper office
   put the reporters' stories
   in shape for the newspaper.
A newspaper has a printing plant.
There the many copies
   of the newspaper are printed
   on big rolls of paper.
(Look up *printing*.)
Newsboys go out
   early in the morning
   or after school
   to deliver newspapers.
They have paper routes.
They take the paper
   to all the houses
   on their routes
   where people want it.
A newsboy may ride
   a bicycle on his route.
Some newsboys stand
   at busy corners
   to sell papers.
They sell them to passersby.
Some people sell newspapers
   at a newsstand.

N

night

Night is dark.
The moon may shine.
Stars may twinkle
   in the dark sky.
There may be lights in houses
   and on streets.
But all around is darkness.
Night is a good time to sleep.

Short-eared Owl

Night is a busy time
   for some people.
Some people work at night.

They go to work when it is dark.
Some animals go about at night.
Cats hunt at night.
Owls and some other birds
   hunt at night, too.
Animals that hunt at night
   can see well in the dark.

Not all the animals
 out at night
 are hunters.

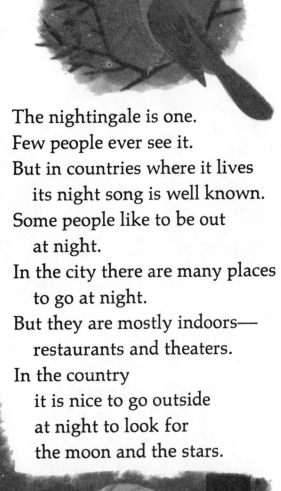

Mice and other small animals
 come out to find seeds
 and other foods.
And some birds sing
 most sweetly at night.

The nightingale is one.
Few people ever see it.
But in countries where it lives
 its night song is well known.
Some people like to be out
 at night.
In the city there are many places
 to go at night.
But they are mostly indoors—
 restaurants and theaters.
In the country
 it is nice to go outside
 at night to look for
 the moon and the stars.

N

nomad

Nomads wander
   from place to place.
Their homes are tents
   they can pack up quickly
   and carry along.
Many families of nomads
   may travel together.

Most nomads live in lands
   where it is hard to grow food.
They live on hot dry deserts
   or in cold barren lands.
They cannot farm there.
So they wander
   from place to place.
They hunt for food
for their families and herds.
(Look up *desert, Eskimo,*
   and *reindeer.*)
Their animals may be goats
   or sheep, camels or ponies.
In the far north, nomads have
   herds of reindeer.

north

Face the setting sun.
Stretch your arms out
    at your sides.
Your right hand
    is pointing north.

Set a compass down on a table.
Wait until its needle
    stops shaking.
The needle is pointing north.
(Look up *magnet*.)
Turn the compass so that N
    is under the needle's point.
The letters tell you
    where the other directions
    are:
        S is for South,
        E is for East,
        W is for West.

The farther north you go,
    the colder it is—
    if you live in the northern half
    of the world.
The north wind can be very cold.
We think of the "North"
    as the land of ice and snow.

Eskimos and polar bears
    live in the far north.
If you keep on going north
    at last you will reach
    the North Pole.
All you will see there
    is ice and snow.

N

note

A note tells us
a little something.
A note may be a sign
that tells us a sound
to play or sing.
A note may be a short letter.

Mother may write a note
to herself about
what she wants to buy.

Sometimes we write notes
in a notebook
or on note paper.

number 123

These are numbers—
0, 1, 2, 3, 4, 5, 6, 7, 8, 9.
We can put these numbers
together
to make a great big number
like 1,234,567,890.
We can put some together
to make a small number
like 12.
We can count things
with numbers.

We can add numbers together.

We can subtract numbers
from one another.

We can do many things
  with numbers.
Doing things with numbers
  is called arithmetic.
People use numbers
  to explain things.

The shoe you wear
  has a number inside.
The number tells its size.

Your house has a number.
The number tells
  where your house is
  on its street.
Highways have numbers.
Your age has a number.
It tells how many years
  you have spent
  learning all you know.

nurse

A nurse cares for babies
  and for sick people.
A nurse learns how to make
  people feel comfortable.
A nurse helps a doctor.
She may work in an office
  or in a school
  or in a hospital.
Wherever she is,
  a nurse is a kind, good friend.

N

nut

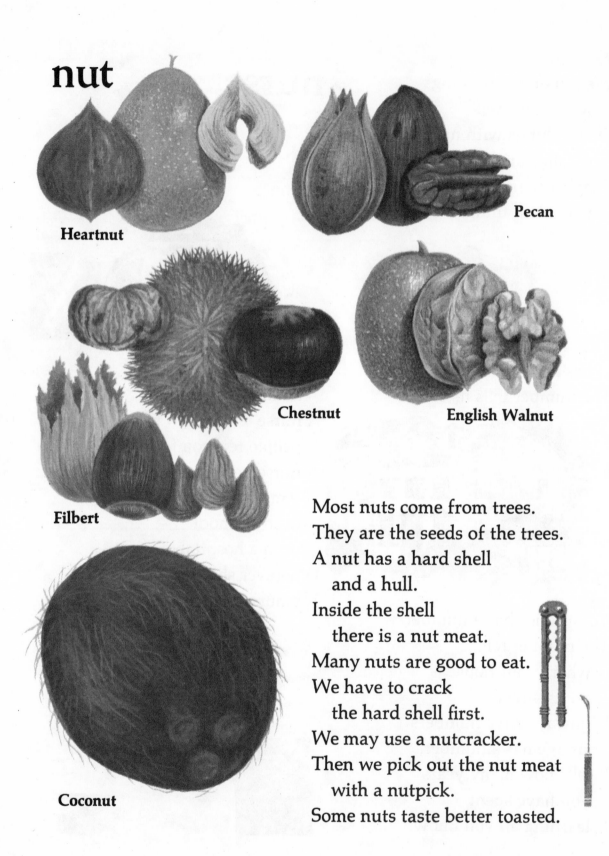

Heartnut

Pecan

Chestnut

English Walnut

Filbert

Coconut

Most nuts come from trees.
They are the seeds of the trees.
A nut has a hard shell
   and a hull.
Inside the shell
   there is a nut meat.
Many nuts are good to eat.
We have to crack
   the hard shell first.
We may use a nutcracker.
Then we pick out the nut meat
   with a nutpick.
Some nuts taste better toasted.

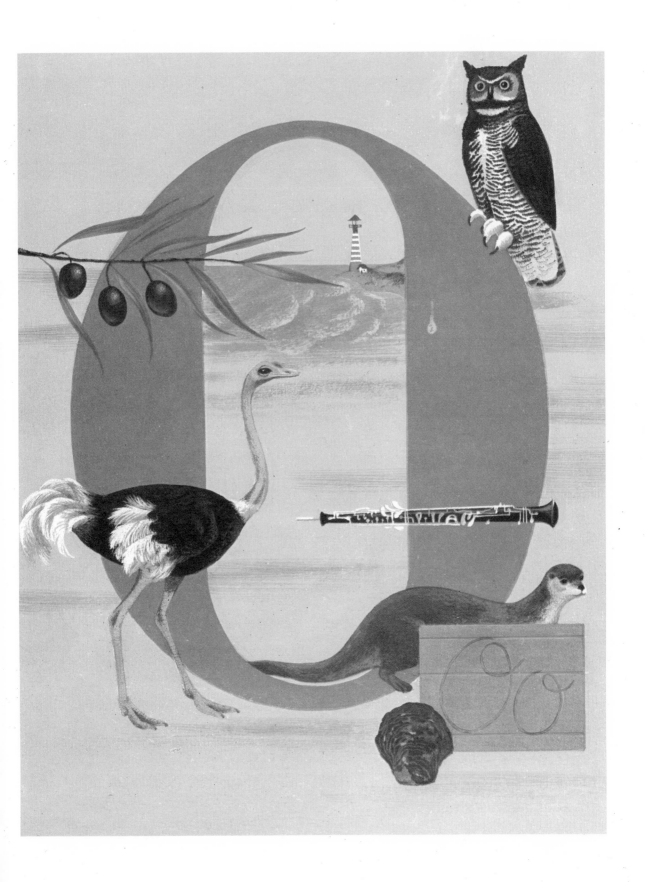

ocean

The ocean covers much of the earth.
Sometimes we call it the sea.
(Look up *sea*.)
We call different parts of the ocean
    by different names—
    the Atlantic Ocean,
    the Pacific Ocean,
    the Indian Ocean,
    the Arctic Ocean,
    the Antarctic Ocean.
But these oceans flow
    into one another.
We cannot tell where one ends
    and another begins.

Ocean liners are "cities afloat."
They have bedrooms,
    living rooms,
      huge kitchens and dining rooms.
They have theaters, shops and
    places for sports.

Big ships and airplanes
    cross the oceans.
One kind of big ship
    that crosses the ocean
    is called an ocean liner.

Some planes that cross the oceans
    are called airliners.
An airliner is not nearly as big
    as an ocean liner.
But it travels much faster.

Where the land meets the ocean,
  the land is called a coast
  or a seashore.
Perhaps it is a sandy beach.
People may have houses there.
They may come in summer
  to swim and sail and watch
  the waves break.
We call waves "breakers"
  when their crests break off
  in foam near the shore.
We call the same kind of waves
  "surf," too.
Some coasts are rocky.
Lighthouses warn ships away.

Many busy towns and cities
  are built on the coast.
A coastal town or city
  must have a harbor
  if ships are to dock there.
(Look up *harbor*.)
Ships come into the harbor
  to unload their cargoes.
Billions of fish
  live in the ocean.
Many of the boats
  that go out from shore
  carry fishermen.
(Look up *fishermen*.)

O

octopus

The octopus lives in the sea
or ocean.
It has a soft body
and eight long arms.
It reaches out its arms to get food.
Its arms have suckers that hold on
tight to what they find.
The octopus can shoot out
an inky fluid
to help it hide
from enemies.

oil

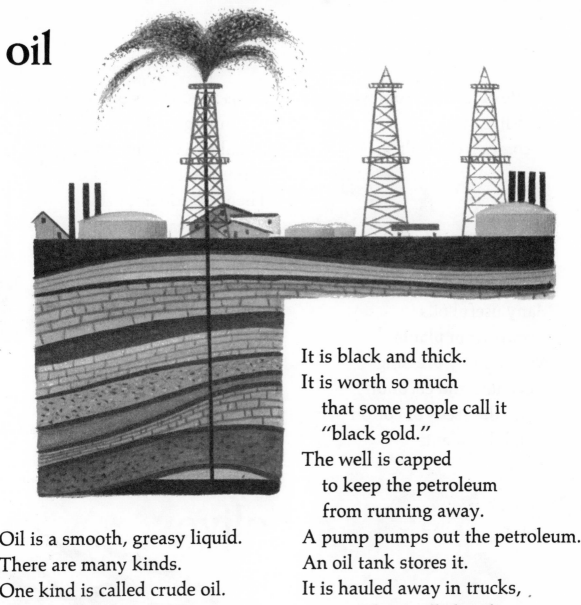

Oil is a smooth, greasy liquid.
There are many kinds.
One kind is called crude oil.
Another name for it is petroleum.
"Petro" means "rock."
Petroleum is found
    by drilling holes
    deep into rock.
These holes are called oil wells.
Sometimes when a hole or shaft
    reaches a pool of petroleum,
    boom! the petroleum shoots up.

It is black and thick.
It is worth so much
    that some people call it
    "black gold."
The well is capped
    to keep the petroleum
    from running away.
A pump pumps out the petroleum.
An oil tank stores it.
It is hauled away in trucks,
    or in ships called tankers
    or in railroad cars
    called tank cars.
In a building called
    an oil refinery,
    the petroleum is made
    into many products.
Not all oil
    comes from petroleum.

O

233

Whale oil comes from whales.
Cod-liver oil
comes from codfish.

Many useful oils
come from plants.
We get oil by pressing
peanuts and coconuts,
and the seeds of cotton plants
and flax plants.

We get oil from corn
and soybeans and olives, too.
We call oils
made from plants
vegetable oils.
Oil is used in making
soaps and paints.
Oil is used in cooking.

Oil is used to keep machines
running well.
It makes a smooth coating
on metal parts.
Then they do not grind
against each other
and wear out so fast.
A few drops of oil
from an oil can
will stop squeaks
and make many things
work better.
An oil can's long spout helps
get the oil where it is needed.
Oiling is called lubrication.

olive

Olives are good to eat
after they are pickled.
They are the fruit
of olive trees.
Olives are often pressed
to squeeze out olive oil.
Olive oil is good
for cooking and in salads.

opera and operetta

An opera is a play
  where most of the words
  are sung.
An orchestra plays all through it.
There is often dancing, too.
An operetta has singing.
It has an orchestra.
It often has dancing.
But part of the time people talk.
They do not sing all the time.

Many schools give operettas.
Boys and girls play the parts
  and sing the songs.
They dress up in costumes.
They wear make-up.
It is called grease paint.
Other boys and girls play
  in the orchestra.
Some help backstage.
Some sell tickets.
Giving an operetta means
  a lot of work.
But it is fun to see one
  or to take part in the work.

o

orchestra

An orchestra is a group
of people playing together
on musical instruments.
Some people play
on stringed instruments.
They move bows
strung with fine hairs
across the strings.
They play violins, violas,
cellos and big double basses.
A double bass is so big
a man has to stand to play it.

Some people play
on woodwinds.
Woodwinds are usually
made of wood.
They are played
by blowing into them
or across an opening.

Some have reeds inside them.
Clarinets, oboes and bassoons do.
Flutes and piccolos do not.
Some people play on brasses.
Brasses are horns made of brass
    that are played by
    blowing into them.
How high or low a horn sounds
    depends on the length
    of its tube.
Some horns have tubes
    that can be stretched out.
Trombones do.
Some horns have tubes so long
    that they are curled
    around and around.

French horns and tubas do.
Some people play
    on percussion instruments.
They beat on drums.
They bang cymbals together.
They strike bars of metal
    with small hammers.
And all the players
    who stroke the strings
    and toot on woodwinds
    and blow into horns
    and beat on drums
    and bang cymbals
    and strike the chimes—
    all the players watch
    the orchestra conductor.
They follow the signals
    the conductor gives them.

O

organ

An organ
  is a musical instrument.
A pipe organ has
  many pipes of many sizes
  to make its sounds.
They are like woodwinds.
But the organist
  does not blow into the pipes.
Air is pumped in.
In old-time pipe organs
  the air was pumped
  into the pipes by hand.
Most pipe organs today
  have electric blowers.
An organist plays the organ
  with his hands and feet.

He pushes keys and pedals.
Pushing a key or a pedal
  lets air into a pipe.
The pipe makes a sound.
The organist also pulls knobs.
The knobs are called stops.
Different stops can make
  the organ sound
  like different instruments
  of the orchestra
  or even like birds.
A reed organ has no pipes.
Its sounds are made
  when air is pushed
  against reeds inside it.
The organist pumps the air
  against the reeds
  with foot pedals.

ostrich

otter

The ostrich is the biggest bird
    there is.
It has long legs.
It can run fast.
Although it has wings,
    it cannot fly.
Sometimes the ostrich is called
    "the camel bird."
It lives in dry country,
    as camels do.
It can go without water
    for days.
It walks rather like a camel,
    too.
Some ostrich feathers are long
    and beautiful.
They are called plumes.

Otters are furry water animals.
Some live in rivers.
Some live in the sea.
Sea otters are larger
    than river otters.
An otter swims and dives.
It can close its ears and nose
    when it is under water.
Often it floats on its back.
An otter may have a meal
    of shellfish
      spread out on its chest
      as it floats about.
A mother sea otter
    may float on her back
    with her baby on her chest.
Otters are very playful.
They seem to have a good time.

O

owl

"Who? Who?" hoots an owl.
It is a lonesome sound.
Some owls do not hoot.
They have other cries.
The hoot owl gets its name
   from its cry.
So does the screech owl.
But the screech owl's cry
   is not really a screech.
Owls call mostly at night.
They hunt food at night.
They can see well in the dark.
As these night birds fly along,
   they can see mice
   running in the grass.
Some owls are rather small.
An elf owl is
   only six inches tall.
Some owls are big.
The great gray owl is
   three feet tall.

oyster

Oysters are animals.
They live fastened tight
   to rocks in the sea.
An oyster has a double shell.
Water with food in it
   flows into the shell.
There are many kinds of oysters.
Pearls and mother-of-pearl
   come from pearl oysters.
(Look up *pearl*.)
People eat oysters
   by the millions.

241

pagoda

A pagoda
   is a special kind of tower.
It is a temple,
   or a part of a temple.
It has an odd number of stories:
   three, five, seven or nine.
Above each story a little roof
   pokes out.
Usually each story is smaller
   than the one below it.
A pagoda may gleam with gold.
It may tinkle with many bells.
We see pagodas in eastern lands
   such as China and Japan.

paint

We use paint to cover
   something with color.
Water colors are paints
   we mix
   with water.
Oil paints

are paints mixed with oil.
We often put on paint
   with a brush
   called a paintbrush.
To paint a small picture
   we use a small brush
   with very fine hairs.
To paint walls
   we use a big brush
   or a roller
   or a spray gun.

Some paints we put on
with just our hands.
We call these paints
finger paints.

painting

A painting is a picture
done in paint.
A person who paints pictures
is called a painter or an artist.

A painting may be done
on a wall.

A painting may be done
on paper
or on cloth called canvas.

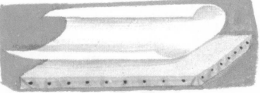

A painting can even be done
on wood or copper.
A painting may show people.

A picture of a real person
is called a portrait.
A picture of a countryside
is called a landscape.
Sometimes a painting
shows just color and shapes.
When a painting is not meant
to look like anything real,
it is called an abstract painting.

palette

paper

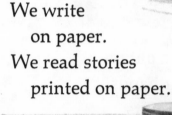

A palette is a board.
A painter holds it in one hand.
He mixes his colors on it.

We write
   on paper.
We read stories
   printed on paper.

panda

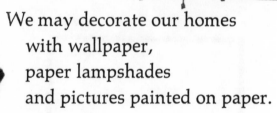

We may decorate our homes
   with wallpaper,
   paper lampshades
   and pictures painted on paper.

We may use paper napkins
   and paper cups and plates.
We carry things in paper bags.
We wrap presents
   in pretty wrapping paper.

Pandas live
   in high mountains.
Giant pandas are like
   furry bears.
They are black and white.
Lesser pandas
   are more like big cats.
They are brown and black.
A few pandas live in zoos.

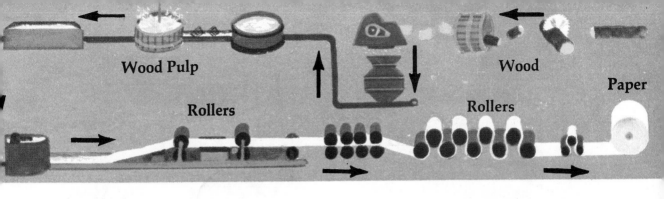

Wood Pulp

Rollers

Wood

Paper

Paper may be made from wood
   or from rags
   or from rice.
Most paper is made from wood.
The wood is cut up fine.
It is boiled to a pulp.
We call this pulp wood pulp.
Wood pulp is a little like
   thin paste.
It is spread on a screen.
The screen has fine holes in it.
Some of the water in the pulp
   drips through the holes.
Most of the rest of it
   is pressed out by big rollers.
A sheet of paper is left.
The paper is then dried
   on rollers.
Most paper is made
   in big paper mills.

But some paper is still made
   by hand.
It usually has rags in it
   to make it stronger
   and finer.

papyrus

Papyrus is a plant.
A lot of it once grew
   in the marshes of Egypt.
People used to split the stems.
They took out the soft pith
   in the centers.
They glued strips of the pith
   together and pressed them
   into flat sheets.
They wrote on these sheets.
Our word "paper"
   comes from "papyrus."

P

parachute

A parachute
 is like
 a great big
 umbrella.

With it a man
 or a tractor
 or a bale of hay
 can float to earth safely
 from an airplane.
In the airplane,
 the parachute is folded up
 into a neat package.
It opens out only in the air.

parakeet and parrot

Parakeets and parrots
 are birds that can learn
 to talk.
They can mimic
 sounds they hear.
Most parrots and parakeets
 come from warm lands.
They have beautiful
 bright feathers.
Some kinds make good pets.

park

A park is an outdoor place
to enjoy.
A city park has trees
and flowers.
It has green grass.
It has paths to walk on
and benches to sit on.
It may have places
to play games.
It may have a playground
with swings and slides.

Many parks have water—
a river, a lake,
a pool or a fountain.

Water helps make a park
beautiful.
Many parks are part garden
There are many big parks
far from big cities.
They may have places to stay
overnight.
People go to these parks
for a vacation.
A park may have a forest.

Or it may have a beach.

A park may have geysers
of hot water
shooting up
from pools underground.
Hot rock deep in the ground
heats the water.

A park may be in the mountains.
It may have beautiful places
to walk and climb.
It may have a waterfall.

A park may be in the desert.
It may have strange plants
for people to see.

A park may have wild animals
that roam free.

A park may have old houses
    where people lived long ago.
It may show how people lived
    back in history.

peanut

Peanuts are seeds.
They are good to eat.
Like peas, they grow in pods.
But peanuts must be dug up.
The stems of a peanut plant,
    as they grow,
    push the pods underground.
Many things are made
    from peanuts.
Peanut oil and meal are two.
But of all the things
    made from peanuts,
    many of us like best
    the good peanut butter
    we spread on bread.

pearl

Pearls are beautiful jewels.
They grow in oyster shells.
(Look up *oyster*.)
A grain of sand
    may be washed into
    an oyster's shell.
The oyster builds a little ball
    of hard material around it.
This ball is a pearl.
Men dive for pearls
    in warm seas.
They bring up oysters
    by the basketful.
They look inside the oysters
    for pearls.

penguin

A penguin is a bird.
It cannot fly.
But it can swim and dive.
It paddles with its wings.
And it can slide on snow.
Most penguins live
near the South Pole.
Emperor penguins live where
there is nothing around
but snow and ice and sea.
The mother penguin
lays one egg.
The father penguin
rests the egg on his feet.
Then he sits on his feet
and on the egg
and keeps them warm
together.

pet

A pet is a tame animal.
It lives with people.
It does not have to work.
People keep a pet
for company and for fun.
Cats and dogs are common pets.

Many people have birds as pets.
Some people have
parakeets that can talk
or canaries that can sing.
Some have pet crows or pigeons.

250

People who have large gardens
    may even have peacocks.
Peacocks do not make
    a pleasant sound.
They screech and scream.

Some people
    keep rabbits
    as pets.
Some keep hamsters
    or guinea pigs
    or white mice.
Some people have
    a lamb for a pet,
    or a baby goat
    or a pony.

But they have very beautiful
    feather "fans" they spread.

Some people have pet fish.
(Look up *aquarium*.)

The important things to know
    if you have a pet
    are how to keep it
    well and happy,
    and how to keep it
    from bothering
    other people.

piano

A piano
   is a musical instrument.
To play it,
   you sit in front of it.
You touch the keys
   on the keyboard—
   black keys and white keys.
When you push down a key,
   inside the piano
   a little hammer
   strikes a long metal string.
The string makes a sound.
You can learn
   to put sounds together
   to make beautiful music
   on a piano.
But it takes lots of practice
   to learn
   to play the piano well.

An upright piano has its strings
   going up and down.
A grand piano has its strings
   going from front to back.

pig

Pigs are farm animals.
They are raised for bacon
   and ham and pork.
Many gloves and purses
   are made from pigskin.

planet

A planet is a huge ball
   of rock and gas.
It travels around the sun.
Our earth is a planet.
There are eight other planets
   that travel around the sun.
Some are larger than the earth.
Some are smaller.
Two are closer to the sun
   than the earth is.
The rest are farther away.
Each planet has its own path
   around the sun.
It travels this path
   over and over and over.

All the planets move
   in the same direction
   around the sun.
The bottom picture shows
   how the sizes of the planets
   compare with one another.
To show in the same scale
   how far the planets are
   from the sun,
   we would need a picture
   much bigger than
   a school playground.
As we look at the sky at night,
   we often see a planet.
It looks like a bright star.
(Look up *star*.)

P

Mercury   Earth   Mars   Venus   Jupiter   Saturn   Uranus   Neptune   Pluto

plant

Milkwort

Plants are living things.
But most of them cannot
 move themselves about
 as most animals can.

Some plants are very tiny.
They are too tiny
 for us to see them easily.
Many of the tiniest plants
 live in the water
 of ponds, lakes or seas.
They have many shapes.

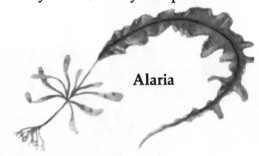

Alaria

Some water plants
 grow quite large.
The largest are big seaweeds.

Most of the plants we know
 have green leaves.
The leaves are factories.
They use sunshine
 to make food
 for the plant.
(Look up *leaf*.)
Trees get their food this way.

Trees are the biggest
 of all plants.

Most plants start from seeds.
All flowering plants
    form seeds.
(Look up *flower*.)

Harebell

Wild Rice

Some plants have other ways
    of starting new plants
    besides forming seeds.

Tulip

Some plants that form seeds
    also have round bulbs
    under the ground.
These bulbs split.
A new plant can grow
    from each new bulb.

Some plants that form seeds
    also send runners
    along the ground.
New roots grow down
    from the runners.

Woodruff

Soon there are new plants
    growing from the new roots.
Some plants form spores
    instead of seeds.
The spores are as tiny
    as specks of dust.
New plants grow
    from the spores.

Marginal Fern

Ferns and mosses
    form spores.   Common
            Meadow Mushroom

So do mushrooms.
(Look up *ferns*,
    mosses and *mushrooms*.)

P

We would not have any food
  without plants.
We eat many plant foods.
Vegetables,
  fruits,
  cereals,
  sugar and spices
  all come from plants.
We eat animal foods too.
But they come from animals
  that eat plants.
Cows give us
  the milk we drink.
Chickens give us
  the eggs we eat.
Pigs and sheep,
  cattle and fowls
  give us meat.
They all eat plants.
We use many things
  made from plants.
Cotton for clothes
  and straw for hats
  come from plants.
Rubber for balls and tires
  comes from rubber trees.
Wood and paper
  come from trees,too.
We could not get along
  without plants!

plastic

Plastics are man-made materials.
They can be given any shape
    while they are warm.
Plastics are not wood or cloth,
    metal or glass,
      rubber, paper, ivory or clay.
But they can take the place
    of these materials.
We have dishes made of plastic
    instead of clay.
They do not break easily.
But they may melt
    if they get too hot!

We have raincoats
    made of plastic
    instead of cloth or rubber.

We have toys made of plastic
    instead of wood.

We have chairs made of plastic
    instead of wood,
    or made of wood
    glued together with plastic.

We have plastic toothbrushes.
We have plastic hairbrushes
    and combs.
We buy food
    and many other things
    in plastic bags
    or wrappings.
We can see what is inside
    the covering
    but what is inside stays clean.
We play plastic records
    on our record players.
Plastics are everywhere,
    clean and bright,
    cheap and light.

P

pony

A pony is a small kind of horse.
A child can ride
    on a pony's back.

Or a pony can pull
    a light pony cart.
Pony Express riders
    carried mail on horseback
    in the early days
    of the American West.
But the horses they rode
    were not really ponies.

potato

A potato plant has
    some stems
    growing underground.
Lumps, or tubers,
    form on these stems.
We call the tubers potatoes.
Potatoes are good to eat.
And new potato plants
    can be grown from them.

president

The president of a country
    is the head
    of the government.
He is chosen by the people.
Most countries today
    have presidents
    or other leaders
    chosen by the people.
In olden times
    the people did not often
    get to choose their leaders.

258

printing

A book is printed.
You may print your name.

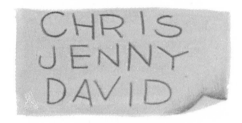

CHRIS
JENNY
DAVID

When you print,
  you use letters that look
  like those in a book.
The letters in a book
  are printed from type.
Type has letters
  shaped in metal.
Printing is done on
  printing presses.
The first printing presses
  were worked by hand.
Some people still use
  hand presses.

A printer puts type letters
  in order.
He spells out words
  in lines of type.
He rubs the type with ink.
He presses paper down on it.
Some ink comes off
  on the paper.
The lines are printed!
Most printing today is done
  on huge machines.
This book was printed
  on a big machine.
It was printed in four colors.
Red, yellow, blue
  and black inks were used.
The colors were pressed
  onto the paper,
  one at a time.

Together they make
  all the colors you see.

P

puppet

A puppet is a doll.
It is a special kind of doll.
It can seem to sing and to dance.
It can seem to walk and to talk.
Of course a person must help
  a puppet move and talk.

If it is a hand puppet,
  you put your hand inside it
  and make it move.
If it is a stringed puppet,
  called a marionette,
  you move the strings.
A person who makes
  a puppet work
  is called a puppeteer.
Some puppets are flat.
They may be made of paper.
They may be made
  of camel skin.
They act behind a sheet.
A light makes their shadows
  show up on the sheet.
Out in front,
  the audience sees
  the shadows move and act.
These puppets are called
  shadow puppets.
A puppet show is fun to see.

puppy

A puppy is a baby dog.
It makes a good pet.

260

quail

Quails are birds.
But they spend more time
    on the ground
    than in the air.
We sometimes see
    a mother quail
    with a whole line of babies
    walking behind her.
If they are frightened,
    they scatter and fly.
But they do not fly far.
Some quails have little "hats"
    of feathers.
Some quails call, "Bob white!"
They are called bobwhites.

quarry

Stone for building
    comes from a quarry.
A quarry is a hole
    dug where there is good stone.
Often the hole is in a hillside.
Men split pieces of stone
    loose from the rock walls.
They lift the stone out
    with cranes.
They haul it away in trucks.

queen

quetzal

The wife of a king is a queen.
Or a queen may be
    the ruler herself.
If a king has no son,
    when he dies his daughter
    may become the queen.
The queen is the most honored
    lady in a kingdom.
Her children are called
    princes and princesses.
Today there are not
    many queens.
There are not many kingdoms
    any more.
(Look up *king*.)

A quetzal is a jungle bird.
It has bright feathers.
It has a long, long tail.
The tail feathers of a quetzal
    may be three feet long.
The quetzal is a beautiful bird.
But it does not live well
    in a cage.
You will seldom see one
    unless you visit the jungles.
Even there, you must be lucky
    to see a quetzal.
Beautiful quetzal feathers
    used to be woven into cloth
    for the robes of kings
    long ago.

Q

quilt

A quilt is a bedcover.
It has a top and a bottom.
Between them is a filling
    of wool, down or cotton.
When the top and bottom
    are stitched together,
    the filling puffs up
    between the stitching.
This stitching is called
    quilting.

Some pretty quilts are made
    of many small pieces
    of different-colored cloth
    sewed together.

It takes a long time
    to make pieced quilts.
But a pieced quilt is
    a pride and joy to own.
In olden days
    women used to work together
    stitching quilts.
They worked and visited
    and sang.
They called this work party
    a quilting bee.

quoits

Quoits is a game.
You set up a peg.
You toss rings at it.
You try to toss the rings
    over the peg.
Quoits is played
    much the same way
    as the game of horseshoes.

rabbit

A rabbit is a small, soft,
   furry animal.
It has long ears
   and a short, fluffy tail.

Rabbits eat
   cabbages and lettuce
   and other plant foods, too.
Wild rabbits make their homes
   in the shelter
   of tree roots
   or thick brush.

Tame rabbits live in cages.
Some are raised for fur.
Some are raised for food.
Some are pets.
Mother rabbits
   have many babies.
They take good care
   of their babies.
They pull soft down
   from their own fur coats
   to line nests
   for their baby bunnies.

radio

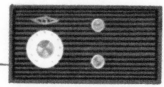

We hear music and voices
  from far away over the radio.
We say a radio program is
  broadcast.
"Broadcast" means
  "thrown in all directions."
Most radio programs start
  in a broadcasting studio.

The entertainers
  speak or sing
  into a microphone.
Or an orchestra plays
  with a microphone
  in front of it.
The speaking, singing,
  or playing
  sets up waves in the air.
We call these waves
  "sound waves."
(Look up *sound*.)

The sound waves affect
  a tiny electric current
  in the microphone.
This electric current
  is made stronger.
It is sent up
  a transmitter tower.
From the tower
  radio waves speed out.
Some of the waves
  strike the antenna
  of your radio set.
They set up an electric current
  in it.
If the radio is turned on
  you can turn a knob
  and tune in to the program.
The sounds you hear
  come from the loudspeaker
  of your radio.
Radio waves travel so fast
  that you can hear a program
  at the very same time
  it is being broadcast!

railroad

A railroad has a road or track
    made of steel rails.
The rails are nailed down
    to wooden beams called ties.

The ties are laid on a bed
    made of gravel and cinders.
Trains run on the track.
Locomotives pull the trains.
(Look up *locomotive*
    and *travel*.)
Some of the trains carry people.
They are passenger trains.

Other trains carry coal and oil,
    fruits and vegetables,
    cattle and machinery.
They carry all sorts of loads.
They are freight trains.
The rims of a train's wheels
    fit over the steel rails
    of the track.

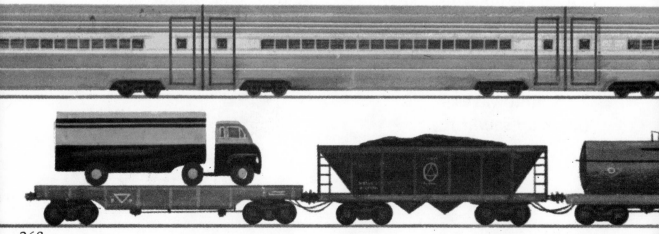

Trains run best
   when the track is smooth
   and level.
When railroad tracks are laid,
   tunnels are dug
   through mountains.

Bridges and trestles are built
   over rivers and deep places.
Embankments are built
   on low, wet land.
All these things help
   to make tracks level.

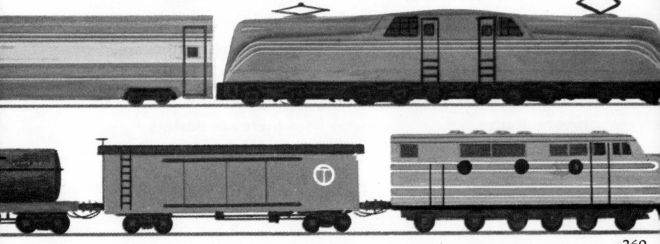

Many trains run
     on the same track.
Here are two trains.
They are coming
     toward each other
     on the same track.
Will there be a wreck?
No.
One train comes to a switch.

Some signals tell him to go slow.
Some tell him to stop.
Some tell him the track
     is clear.
Some signals have colored arms.
They are called semaphores.
Some signals have colored lights.
Signals help keep the trains
     running safely.

It will be switched off
     onto a short side track
     called a siding.
The track will be clear
     for the other train.
Soon the first train
     will back up
     onto the main track again
     and go chugging on its way.
There are signals
     along the track.
Signals tell the engineer
     of a train
     what to do.

The men who work on a train
     are called the train crew.
There is a fireman
     to help the engineer.
There are brakemen
     and conductors.
If it is a passenger train
     and there is a dining car,
     there are waiters and cooks.
And there is a steward in charge.
If there are sleeping cars,
     there are porters
     to take care of them.

Some railroad men
    keep the track in good shape.
They are called section hands.

Some railroad men
    work in the stations.
They take care of baggage
    and tickets.

Some railroad men
    look after railroad cars
    and locomotives
    between runs.
These men work
    in the railroad yards.

A railroad yard
    is full of tracks.
It has many switches
    and sidings.
It has small switch engines
    to move cars around.
It has turntables, too.

The turntables
    turn locomotives around.
A locomotive is driven
    onto a turntable.
The "table" turns around
    with the locomotive on it
    until it heads
    in the right direction.
The turntable may be
    in a building called
    a roundhouse.
Locomotives stay
    in the roundhouse
    until their next run.
A railroad has many, many
    kinds of work
    for railroad men to do.

R

rain

Rain falls from clouds.
A rain cloud is made of water.
The water is in tiny droplets.
Sometimes many tiny droplets
    gather into a big drop.
The drop is too heavy
    to float in the cloud.
It falls to earth.
It is a drop of rain.
If raindrops fall
    through very cold air,
    they may freeze.
They fall to earth
    as sleet.
If the air around a cloud
    is very, very cold,
    ice crystals form
    instead of raindrops.
They fall to earth as snow.

Plants need water
    to help them stay alive
    and grow.
The roots of a plant
    get the water
    the plant needs
    from the ground.

Where rain falls or snow melts
    water soaks into the ground.
It is ready for plants to use.
Where there is very little rain
    and no other way
    of getting water,
    few plants grow.
The ground is too dry
    for most plants.
We say the land is a desert.
(Look up *desert*.)
But it can rain too much.
Then there may be a flood.
(Look up *flood*.)
Rain can be good or bad.
It is not good for a picnic!

rainbow

We often see a rainbow
   if it rains
   while the sun is out.
All the colors of the rainbow
   are in sunlight.
When sunlight falls
   on raindrops,
   its colors separate.
We see them arch in bands
   across the sky.
The order of the colors
   is always the same—
   red
   orange
   yellow
   green
   blue
   violet.

Sometimes we can see
   a rainbow in the spray
   of a water sprinkler
   or a waterfall.

rain clothes

It is fun
   to go out in the rain.
But when we do,
   it is best to be dressed
   for the rain.
Rubbers
   or boots
   keep our feet dry.

Rain hats
   or plastic hoods
   keep our heads dry.
Raincoats
   keep most of
   our clothing dry.
Some raincoats
   are called ponchos.
You pull a poncho
   over your head
   to put it on.
When it rains, some people
   carry umbrellas
   to keep the rain off.

R

ranch

A ranch is a big farm
   for raising cattle or sheep.
On a cattle ranch,
   cowboys look after
   the cattle.
The cattle wander
   over the land, eating grass.
(Look up *cattle and cows.*)
We call this
   grazing on the range.
Cowboys often ride the range
   to see that the cattle
   are safe and healthy.

When calves are born,
   the cowboys
   must brand them.
A brand is the mark
   of the ranch.

The cowboys stamp the brand
   onto the calf's skin
   with a hot iron.
Then if the calf gets lost,
   people can always tell
   what ranch it belongs to.
The brand tells them.

Sometimes cowboys camp out
   on the range.
They have a chuck wagon
   that carries their food
   and a cook
   to cook their meals.
When the cowboys
   are not riding the range,
   they live in a bunkhouse.
They keep their horses
   in a big pen
   called a corral.

The rancher and his family
   live in the ranch house.
The rancher decides
   when to send cattle
   to market.
Then the cowboys herd them
   into a shipping pen.
The cattle walk up
   onto a platform
   and into a truck.
   or into the cattle car of a train.
And off to market they go.
For the cattle rancher's business
   is raising cattle to sell.
A ranch where people
   pay to come
   and spend their vacation
   is called a dude ranch.
There are many ranches
   in the West.

R

record

We play records
on a record player.
Sounds are recorded
on a record
by a recording needle.
The needle cuts a wavy groove
around the record.
If we want to hear the sounds,
we set the record
spinning on the turntable
of a record player.
We place the record player's
needle onto the record.
It fits into
the record's grooves.
Then the record player
plays the sounds
which were recorded.
Music or voices
or any sort of sound
can be on a record.
Records are sometimes called
"discs" or "platters"
because they are round
and flat.

refrigerator

A refrigerator keeps food cold.
Keeping food cold
helps keep it from spoiling.
Years ago, the only refrigerators
were iceboxes.
The iceman put ice
in the icebox.
As the ice melted,
it cooled the food
in the icebox.
Now our refrigerators are run
by electricity or gas.
They have a special liquid
in the working part.
The liquid turns to gas,
then back to liquid,
over and over again.
Each time it turns to gas
it cools the food.

reindeer

Reindeer live
   in the ice and snow
   of the far north.
They live in herds.
Reindeer help people.
They furnish milk to drink,
   and meat to eat,
   and skins to wear.
They pull heavy loads
   over the snow.
Stories say that reindeer
   pull Santa Claus' sleigh
   on Christmas Eve.

Lapland

reptile

A reptile is an animal.
It may have short legs.
Or it may have no legs at all.

Snakes are reptiles
   that have no legs.
They wriggle over the ground.

Lizards are reptiles.
Most lizards have short legs.
They can move very fast.

Turtles are reptiles
   that have hard shells.
Some are called tortoises.

Alligators and crocodiles
   are reptiles, too.

R

Reptiles are not warm-blooded
   like birds and furry animals.
The reptiles that live
   where winters are cold
   must find a place to sleep
   during the cold weather.
When they sleep
   through the winter
   we say they are hibernating.
Today reptiles are not
   as important
   as they once were.

Millions and millions
   of years ago,
   they were the leading
   animals on earth.
We call that time
   the Age of Reptiles.
Many of the reptiles of long ago
   were dinosaurs.
(Look up *dinosaur*.)
Some reptiles swam in the sea.
There were even reptiles
   that flew through the air.

rhinoceros

Indian Rhinoceros

The rhinoceros is big
and clumsy looking.
Of all four-legged animals,
only the hippopotamus
and the elephant
are bigger.
The rhinoceros has
one or two sharp horns
sticking up on its nose
It has thick skin.
It lives where it is hot.
The rhinoceros
cannot see very well.
But it has a good sense of smell
and very good hearing.

African Rhinoceros

rice

Rice is a food.
It comes from a rice plant.
We eat the seeds
of the rice plant.
Rice grows well
in a lot of water.
Water is kept standing
in the fields
where rice is grown.

These fields of rice
are called paddies.
They have low walls
around them
to hold the water in.
Small rice plants are set
into the wet fields by hand.
When the rice is ripe,
the water is drained out.
In many countries
rice is the food
that people eat
every day.

R

river

A river is
  a large stream of water
  running downhill
  on its way to the sea.
Many little streams
  join to make a river.
A river wears away
  the earth it flows over
  and makes itself a valley.
Water runs fast
  when it runs down
  a steep hill
  or a mountain.

It can pick up sand
  and pebbles
  and bits of earth
  and carry them along.
It can roll boulders.
As it moves earth and rocks,
  a fast-flowing river
  digs its valley
  deeper and deeper.

It may dig a deep canyon.

Some rivers run
   through almost level land.
They do not run as fast
   as those that run
   down steep slopes.
They slowly wear away
   the banks
   along their sides.
Their valleys
   grow wider and wider.
Wide, slow rivers
   are easy for boats
   to travel on.
Rivers are often called
   "water highways"
   because so many boats
   travel on them.
The boats carry people.
They carry goods to market.

Many cities are built
   beside busy rivers.
When a river
   runs into the sea
   it drops its load
   of earth and sand
   and pebbles
   picked up from the land.
Sometimes the load
   a river carries
   is washed far out to sea.
Sometimes it piles up
   on the bottom of the sea
   at the river's mouth.
In time it reaches
   above the water
   and becomes dry land.
This new land
   is called a delta.

R

road

A road is a broad path
   for cars or carts
   to travel on.
Some country roads
   are not used much.
No special surface or topping
   is put on them.
They are just dirt roads.
They may have deep ruts
   cut by the car
   or cart wheels.
People work on other roads
   to make them smooth.
They put a surface on them
   so that they will not
   get too muddy
   when it rains.
Many roads have
   crushed stone on top.
The rain goes
   through this surface
   and leaves it dry.

Some early roads
   through the woods
   had logs for a surface.

These roads were called
   corduroy roads.
They were bumpy!
But even long, long ago
   some good roads were made.

They were paved
   with large, flat stones.
Later some roads
   and city streets
   were paved with bricks.

Roads paved with stone
   or brick were all right
   for horses and wagons
   and for marching men.

But they are not good
   for automobiles.
With automobiles
   people traveled
   faster and farther.
And every year there were
   more and more automobiles.
We needed
   more and better roads.
Now most of our roads and
   streets are paved with
   concrete or with blacktop.

Concrete is poured
   on a smooth bed
   of crushed stone.
The poured concrete is thick
   and wet and white.
It dries hard and smooth.

Blacktop is also spread
   on a smooth bed
   of crushed stone.
It is thick and hot and sticky.
Heavy rollers press it flat
   and smooth.
When it dries
   there is a very good road.

Busy main roads
   are called highways.
(Look up *highway*.)
Many trucks and automobiles
   travel on them.
We say the traffic is heavy.
(Look up *traffic*.)

R

robin

Robins are friendly birds.
They live near people.
A robin is often
    the first bird we see
    in spring
    that we did not see
    in winter.
We know the robin
    by its reddish breast.
Robins build their nests
    of sticks and leaves,
    bits of string,
    grass and mud.

A robin's nest
    may not be beautiful.
But it is strong.
The mother bird lays her eggs
    in the nest.
The eggs are pale blue-green.
We call this color
    "robin's egg blue."
Hungry baby robins hatch
    from the eggs.

rock

Rock is the stuff
    the earth's crust
    is made of.
Much of it is in big
    masses or layers.
But some is in small pieces.
Solid rock is so hard,
    it seems as if
    it could never be changed.
But it is changed.
Water carrying bits of rock
    can break up big rocks.

Waves eat away rock cliffs
    beside a lake or sea.
Rivers cut their way down
    through solid rock.

Wind carrying sand
   can carve rock
   into strange shapes.
Glaciers can grind up rock.
(Look up *glacier*.)
Rock is always
   being worn away,
   slowly, slowly.
But slowly, slowly,
   new rock is made.

On the bottom of the sea,
   layers of mud and sand
   with pebbles and shells
   in them are built up.
In time these layers
   become solid rock
   of different kinds.
Fiery-hot liquid rock oozes up
   through cracks from
   deep in the earth.
Some of it cools
   underground.
It hardens into rocks
   of other kinds.

Some of the hot, liquid rock
   pours out of volcanoes.
We call it lava.
It hardens into still
   other kinds of rock.

There are many, many
   different kinds of rock.

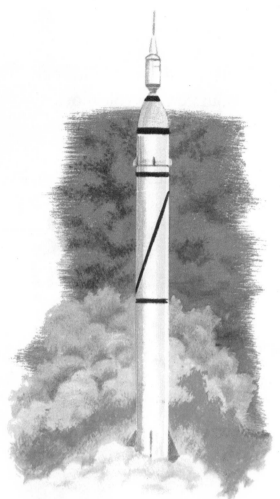

rocket

A rocket is a long tube.
It can be made to rise
 high into the air.
Fuel is burned
 inside the rocket
 to make gas.
Some of the hot gas
 shoots out the back
 of the rocket.
Some pushes forward inside.
It pushes the rocket ahead.

Fourth of July skyrockets
 have paper tubes.
Inside is a powder to burn
 and form gas.
When the skyrocket
 is high in the sky,
 another powder lights.
When it burns,
 it looks like colored stars.
Big rockets can go into space.
Many big rockets have tubes
 made up of sections.
One section burns its fuel
 and drops off.
Then the next section
 does the same, and so on.
The top of a big rocket
 is the most important part.
It is called the payload.
The payload
 may be a warhead.
It may be a satellite.
It may even be
 a space capsule
 with an astronaut inside.
(Look up *satellite*
 and *space*.)

rodeo

A rodeo
   is a cowboy show.
The cowboys do fancy riding
   on horses and bulls.
They do fancy roping.
Cowboys pay to enter a rodeo.
If they win contests,
   they win money prizes.
A rodeo is a lively show.

rose

A rose is a pretty flower.
It may be red or pink,
   yellow or white.
It may grow on a tall vine.
It may grow on a low bush.
Most kinds of roses have
   sharp thorns on their stems.

A rose may grow wild
   and have five petals.
It may be grown in a garden
   and have many more
   than five petals.
Gardeners give their roses
   special food and care.
The rose belongs to a big family
   called the rose family.
Apples, pears, peaches,
   cherries, strawberries
   and many other plants
   belong to the rose family, too.

R

rubber

Rubber got its name
  because it could rub out
  pencil marks.
Rubber can stretch.
Rubber bounces.
Rubber is strong.
All rubber used to come
  from rubber trees.
Today much of it is made
  from oil or gas.
But a lot of natural rubber
  is still used.
To get this rubber,
  men make cuts
  in the bark
  of rubber trees.
The juice,
  called sap,
  runs out.

Men catch the sap
  in cups.
They pour it into tanks
  to thicken.

They make it into balls
  or sheets of rubber.
Then they send it to factories
  where it is made usable.
Rubber is used in
  tires for automobiles,
  airplanes, tractors
  and bicycles.
We have rubber balls,
  or balls with rubber
  inside them.
(Look up *ball*.)
There are rubber hoses
  and boots
  and balloons.
Rubber is used
  in many, many ways.

289

saddle

You sit on a saddle
  to ride a tricycle
  or a bicycle
  or a horse.

A saddle for a horse
  has stirrups
  to hold your feet.
You may hang
  a pair of saddlebags
  from a horse's saddle.
You can pack things
  in saddlebags.

safety

When something suddenly
  goes wrong,
  we say there is an accident.
Someone may start a fire
  without meaning to,
  or have a bad fall.
Or one automobile
  may hit another.
No one wants an accident
  to happen.
Safety rules are to keep us
  from having accidents.
If everyone obeyed them,
  there would be
  fewer accidents.
Here are some safety rules:
1. Pick up your toys.
Someone may fall over them.

2. Do not play with matches.

Matches can start bad fires.

3. Do not climb too high.
You may have a bad fall.

4. Do not play with
electric wires and plugs.
You may get a shock.

5. Look both ways
before crossing the street.
If a car is coming, wait.

6. Obey the policeman
or crossing guard.

7. Do not go swimming
without a grownup.
8. Do not play with
medicine bottles.

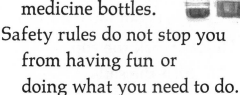

Safety rules do not stop you
from having fun or
doing what you need to do.
You can play with toys.
You can cross streets.
You can turn on lights.
You can go swimming.
You can take medicine
when you need it.
But safety rules tell you
how to do things safely.
If you follow the rules
you will be more likely
to stay happy and well.

S

sailboat

A sailboat needs wind.
The wind pushes the sails.
Then the sails
   pull the boat along,
   and we go sailing.
A sailboat may be very small.
One person can sail
   a very small boat.
He can work the ropes
   to turn the sails.
He can push the rudder
   to steer the boat.

Every sailboat
   must have a sail
   and a mast to hold the sail.
A big sailing ship has
   two or three masts.
It has many sails.
It needs more than one sailor
   to sail it.
A big sailing ship
   can sail across the ocean.
(Look up *boat, ship*.)

salt

To stay well, our bodies
　　need some salt.
Salt makes food taste better.
Table salt is made up
　　of tiny, hard, white crystals.
Salt is a mineral.
Some salt
　　is found underground.
Men dig it out of salt mines.
There is salt in sea water
　　and in the water
　　of salt lakes, too.

In some places, men pump
　　water from the sea
　　into pools near the shore.
The sun dries up the water.
Salt is left.

sand

Sand is rock
　　that has been broken up
　　into tiny grains.
Wind and water
　　and freezing cold
　　help break up rock into sand.
There are beaches of sand.
There are great deserts of sand.
Water can move sand.
Wind can pile sand
　　into low hills.

We call these hills sand dunes.
We may play with sand
　　in a sand box.
(Look up *desert*
　　and *rock*.)

S

sandpiper

A sandpiper is a bird.
It lives on beach sands.
It has a piping call.

satellite

A satellite travels
 around a planet.
(Look up *planet*.)

The earth is a planet.
The moon travels
 around the earth.
The moon is a satellite
 of the earth.

Men can make satellites.
They make satellites
 that circle the earth.
Men put radios
 into their satellites.

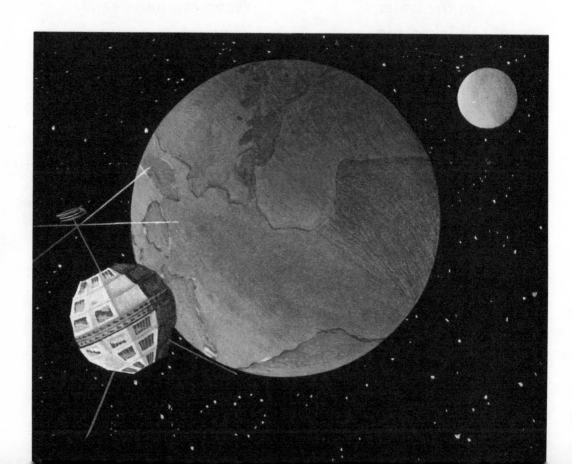

To send a satellite into space,
    men put it into the nose
    of a huge rocket.
Or they fit the satellite
    onto a rocket.
Then they send the rocket
    shooting into space.
(Look up *rocket*
    and *space*.)
When the rocket
    gets way out in space,
    it falls away and
    leaves the satellite by itself.

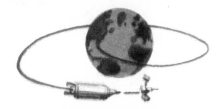

The satellite then travels
    in a path around the earth.
Its radios send information
    from out in space.
(Look up *radio*.)
Men on earth
    tune in on the radio waves
    coming from the satellite.
They get the information.
Some satellites sent traveling
    around the earth
    carry men inside them.

saw

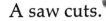

A saw cuts.
A saw has "teeth"
    in its blade.
The teeth are the cutting part
    of the saw.
A hand saw may be so big
    it takes two men
    to push it back and forth.
An electric saw is driven
    by an electric motor.

A big saw like this
    is used to cut big trees.
A saw is usually used
    to cut wood.
But a saw can cut
    other things, too.
A butcher uses a saw
    to cut bones.
A saw blade may be a circle.
As the blade spins,
    it cuts.
This kind of saw is called
    a circular saw.
A saw is a tool.
Learn to use it right so that
    you will not be hurt by it.

S

scales

school

We weigh things on scales.
Scales tell us
    how heavy things are.
(Look up *weight*.)
Some scales are spring scales.
We step onto spring scales
    to weigh ourselves.
A spring inside the scale moves.
Then a pointer on the scale
    shows the right number
    of pounds.
Food is weighed
    on spring scales, too.
Some scales are balances.
A balance is a bar
    with two pans on it.
In one pan you put
    what you want to weigh.
In the other pan
    you put metal weights.
When the pans balance,
    you add up the weights.

We go to school to learn.
We learn to read and write
    and work with numbers.
We learn about plants and
    animals and stars
    and clouds.
We learn about our own
    country and about other
    countries, too.
We sing and paint and
    play games.
We learn to work and play
    together.
It takes many years for us to
    learn all we need to know.

Day is when we give thanks
and school and everything

Some children
    start going to school
    when they are only three.
They go to nursery school.
They play games together.

After nursery school comes
    kindergarten.
These kindergarten children
    are watching a hen and some
    baby chickens.

Not all children go to nursery
school or kindergarten.
But we all go to first grade
when we are six.
These children are in
first grade.

These boys and girls are in the
fourth grade.

They are experimenting
with magnets.
After the sixth grade come the
seventh and eighth grades.
The seventh and eighth grades
are sometimes called
junior high school.
After the eighth grade comes
high school.

One is showing her pet poodle
to the others and is telling
about it.
After first grade
comes second grade.
And then come third grade and
fourth grade and fifth grade
and sixth grade.
Each grade takes a year.
Every year there are new things
to learn.

These high-school girls
are playing basketball.

These pupils
    are studying
    in the high-school library.
High-school boys and girls
    must study hard.
High school takes three or
    four years.
Some boys and girls stop going
    to school when they finish
    high school.
But some go to trade schools.
And some go to a college or
    a university.

These are some of the buildings
    of a college.

Even after they are grown up,
    many people keep on going
    to school.
They may go to night schools.
They may go to school in
    vacation time.
There is always more to learn.
Some of the schools in other
    lands do not look much like
    the schools in our country.

These Lapland children are
    learning to use an abacus
    for arithmetic.
These Arab children are
    learning to read.

Many children learn to write
    on painted boards
    instead of on paper.
All over the world there are
    schools where people learn.

science

Science is all that we find out
   by studying
   the world around us.
The men and women
   who do the studying
   are called scientists.

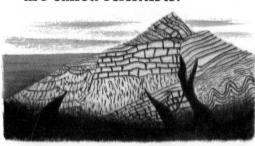

Some scientists study
   the rocks of the earth
   and how they change.
Some study the waters
   of the oceans
   and how the waters move.

Some study the plants
   that live in water.
Some study the fish
   and other animals
   that live in water.

Some study the plants and
   animals that live on land—

big ones and small ones.

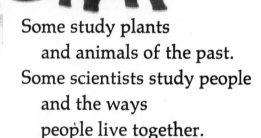

Some study plants
   and animals of the past.
Some scientists study people
   and the ways
   people live together.

Some scientists study
   clouds and winds and storms.

Some scientists study the stars
   and the huge stretches
   of outer space.

Some scientists study
    tiny bits of matter
    called atoms.
They may try to find out
    how these tiny bits of matter
    are put together
    to make rocks and water,
    air and living things.
Scientists look carefully
    at the world around them.
They look at the sky
    through telescopes.
They look at very small things
    under microscopes.

They often work in workrooms
    called laboratories.
Scientists have to do
    a great deal
    of careful measuring.
Scientists never
    run out of things to do.
There is always more to learn
    in science.

sculpture

Take some modeling clay.
Make an animal with it.
Or carve a figure
    from a cake of soap.
You are doing sculpture.
Sculpture is the art
    of forming shapes
    by modeling or carving.
Some sculptors carve
    wood or stone.
Some make shapes
    from clay or metal.
Some pieces of sculpture
    are very large.

S

sea

There is more sea than land
  on this earth of ours.
The water in the sea is salty.
The edges of land along the sea
  are called seashores
  or seacoasts.
There may be a beach
  on a seashore.

Sea gulls fly over the sea.
They swoop down
  to catch fish.
They lay their eggs
  on the beach.

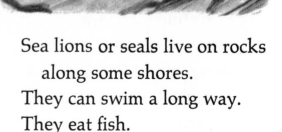

We find sea shells
  on the beach.
Sea animals called shellfish
  once lived in these shells.

Sea lions or seals live on rocks
  along some shores.
They can swim a long way.
They eat fish.

Seaweeds are sea plants.
They grow under the water.

Many kinds of fish live
in the sea.

Sea horses are fish.
They can hold on to seaweed
by curling their tails
around it.

Some have long stems
that may grow up
to the top of the sea.
They have soft, slippery
leaflike parts.
Seaweeds are also called algae.
Some are good to eat.

S

seasons

A season
   is a part of the year.
In many parts
   of the world
   there are four seasons.
They are spring, summer,
   fall and winter.

Summer is the growing season.
Plants grow.
Flowers bloom.
Seeds ripen.
Farmers harvest crops.
Baby birds and
   other animals grow.
People take time to swim and
   have picnics and take trips.

Spring is the season
   when things begin to grow.
The weather warms up
   after winter.
Trees put out new leaves.
Grasses and many other plants
   send up new stems
   and leaves.
Many baby animals
   are born in the spring.

When fall comes, school starts.

Fall or autumn
    may be a beautiful season.
Leaves turn beautiful colors.
Many days are bright and cool.
The sun is not as hot
    as it is in summer.
Nights grow colder.
Late in the fall
    many plants die.

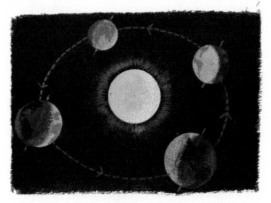

Winter is a season of rest.
Trees rest from growing.
Seeds wait for spring.
Some animals sleep.
Snow falls.
The days are short
    and cold.
But winter brings us
    merry Christmastime.
And after winter
    spring comes again.

Our seasons change
    as the earth circles the sun.
(Look up *planet*.)
Sometimes our part of the earth
    is tipped toward the sun.
We get a lot of sunshine then.
We get a lot of heat.
We have summer.
When our part of the earth
    is tipped away from the sun,
    we get less sunshine.
We get less heat.
We have winter.
Some lands do not have
    a cold season.
They are warm all year.
Their seasons may be
    a wet season
    and a dry season.
Near the North Pole
    and the South Pole
    it is cold the year around.

S

seed

Elm

A seed is part of a plant.
A new plant can grow
    from a seed.
(Look up *flower*
    and *plant*.)
A seed has a baby plant inside
    with one or two tiny leaves.
A seed may be as small
    as a grain of dust.
But it still has
    a tiny plant inside.
There is some food inside
    for the tiny plant, too.
There is a seed coat
    around the little plant
    and its food.
In a warm, damp place
    the seed coat will soften.

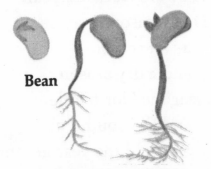

Bean

The baby plant will push out.

Seeds cannot move
    by themselves.
But most seeds can travel.
Some fly on the wind.

Maple

They have wings
    or parachutes.

Cocklebur

Some seeds ride in animals' fur.

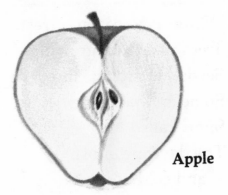

Apple

Some seeds are hidden
    in fruits.
Animals that eat the fruits
    may carry
    the seeds to new homes.

Lotus

Some seeds float on water.

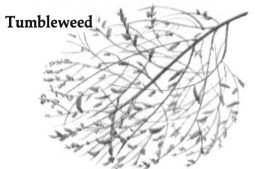

Tumbleweed

Some roll along the ground.

Some seeds are buried
     by animals.
Squirrels often bury nuts.
If a squirrel buries a nut
     and forgets to eat it,
     a tree may grow
     from the nut.
Every seed may grow
     into a plant, given a chance.

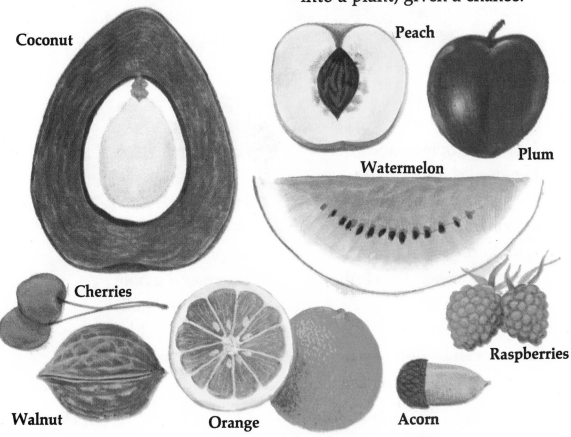

Coconut

Peach

Plum

Watermelon

Cherries

Raspberries

Walnut

Orange

Acorn

S

sewing

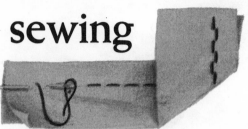

We sew cloth
  with a needle and thread.
The hole in the needle
  that the thread goes through
  is called an eye.

We may sew
  on a sewing machine.
Most of our clothes are sewed
  on sewing machines.
The needle
  on a sewing machine,
  like other needles,
  has a point
  to go through the cloth.
It also has an eye
  for the thread.
Sewing can be done faster
  with a sewing machine
  than by hand.

Every time the thread
  goes in and out
  of the cloth
  it makes what we call
  a stitch.
We can make fancy stitches.

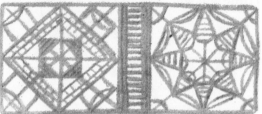

We may sew pretty patterns
  with white thread or with
  thread of different colors.
We call patterns made
  with stitches embroidery.

Mending holes by sewing
  is called darning
  or patching.
If you mend a hole
  when it is small,
  it will not get large.
For this reason people say,
  "A stitch in time
  saves nine."

sheep

Sheep are animals
   with woolly coats.
Wool is made from their coats.
(Look up *wool*.)
Most sheep are tame.
They wander in flocks.
They eat grass.

In many places,
   shepherds look after them.
Baby sheep
   are called lambs.

shell

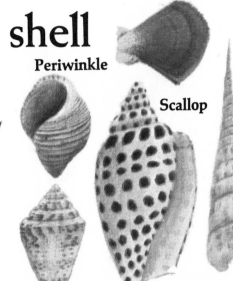

Periwinkle

Scallop

Auger

Cone

Volute

Murex

Sunray

Star

Many water animals
   have shells
   instead of bones.
We often find their shells
   on lake and sea shores.
Some land animals
   have shells, too.
Some shells are in one piece.
Some are in two pieces
   that fit together.
Many shells are pretty.

S

ship

A ship goes to sea.
It is bigger than a boat.
It may be a steamship.
A steamship has engines.
The engines turn propellers.
The propellers push
   the ship through the water.
(Look up *aircraft*
   for more about propellers.)
A big steamship
   may be an ocean liner
   that carries people
   across the ocean.
An ocean liner
   is a floating hotel.
(Look up *ocean*.)

A ship may be a freighter
   that carries goods.
It may be a navy ship.
(Look up *navy*.)

The old sailing ships look small
    beside ships of today.
But in the sailing ships of old
    brave men sailed the seas.

Before the days of steamships
    all ships
    were sailing ships.
The very early ones had
    oars as well as sails.
When there was no wind
    to fill the sails,
    men pulled on
    the oars
    to make the ships go.

They visited unknown lands.
Brave men in small sailing ships
    found America.

S

shoes

Most of the shoes we wear
   are made of leather
   or of cloth.
Others are made of grass,
   wood, rubber or plastic.
High shoes
   are often called boots.

Cowboys wear boots.

Boots are good to wear
   for riding horseback.

Some fishermen wear
   high wading boots
   for keeping dry.

On cold or rainy days we may
   wear boots called overshoes.

Shoe soles with only straps
   to hold them on
   are called sandals.
Sandals are very cool
   and light.
They are good to wear
   when it is hot.
Around the house
   we may wear
   soft shoes called slippers.

312

shop

A shop is a place
  where things are sold
  or made.
We go shopping to buy things.
Workmen make many things
  in workshops.

power shovel

A power shovel
  has a very large scoop
  and a very long handle.
It has an engine
  to give it power.
A power shovel digs
  very large holes
  for new buildings
  or new roads.

shovel

snow shovel

A shovel has a scoop
  and a handle.
Shovels are used
  for picking up and moving
  earth, sand, snow
  and other things.
We can do some digging
  with a shovel.

sand shovel

shower

Water falls
  in a shower.
It may fall from a cloud.
(Look up *rain*.)
It may fall from
  a shower bath.
A shower
  usually falls
  lightly.

S

signal

Ships signal
  to other ships.

A signal gives news.
Or it tells someone
  what to do.
A policeman signals
  with his hand
  for cars to stop — or go.

They signal with flags
  and lights
  and radio.

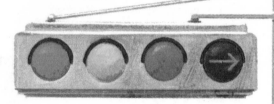

A trainman signals
  with a lantern
  for the train
  to start or wait.

Traffic lights
  are signals.
So are the lights
  on lighthouses.
Your mother may signal
  with a wave of her arm
  when she wants you
  to come.
Your father may signal
  with a shake of his head
  when he wants you to stop.
You know their signal language
  and understand.

Some people signal
  by beating
  on drums.
Others blow horns.
Some people signal
  with fire
  or smoke.

silver

silk

Silk comes from cocoons
  silkworms spin.
Silkworms are the
  caterpillars of certain moths.
Silkworms feed
  on mulberry leaves.
Then they spin cocoons.
When they come out
  of the cocoons
  they are full-grown moths.
Many cocoons are gathered
  before the moths come out.
These cocoons are cooked
  until they are soft.
Their fine soft thread
  is unwound.
Several of the fine threads
  are spun together
  to make stronger ones.
Then many of them are woven
  into silk cloth.
(Look up *cloth*.)

Silver is a metal.
It is shiny.
And it is soft for a metal.
Mix one part copper
  with nine parts silver.
You have sterling silver.
It is harder than pure silver.

It makes beautiful knives,
  forks and spoons.

It makes beautiful bowls,
  platters and teapots.
And it is used in coins.
Silver makes jewelry, too.
But it gets dark easily.
We say it tarnishes.
Then it must be polished.

skeleton

Many animals have bones.
Their bones make up
   their skeletons.
(Look up *bone*.)
A skeleton gives an animal
   its shape.
Some of the bones
   of the skeleton
   protect soft parts.
The bones we call ribs
   make a sort of cage
   for the soft parts inside.
The skull is a thick box
   of bone.
It protects the brain
   and eyes and ears.
And the bones of the skeleton
   help the animal move.

sky

The sky is
   all around the earth.

In the daytime
   the sky looks blue.
(Look up *day*.)
The air scatters
   the blue color
   from the sunlight
   all over the sky.
That is why the sky looks blue.
Water looks blue
   because it mirrors
   the blue sky.

We may see clouds in the sky.
(Look up *cloud*.)
At the end of the day,
    the sun shining on clouds
    gives us a lovely sunset.
Then the sun disappears.
The sky darkens.
We say night falls.

Now we can see stars
    and sometimes the moon.
In the daytime
    bright sunlight
    hides the stars from us.
Sometimes we can see
    the moon in the daytime.
But then it is very pale.
(Look up *moon*
    and *star*.)

S

smoke

Smoke rises from a fire.
When anything burns,
  it turns into something new.
Wood turns into ashes
  and gases.
The smoke from the wood
  is made mostly of the gases.
Some smoke is white.
But smoke may have
  bits of ash
  and soot in it.
They make it gray or black.
Gray smoke from factories
  may make a city dirty.
If it mixes with fog,
  it helps make smog.

snail

A snail is a small,
  soft animal
  that has a hard shell.
The shell is coiled up.
Some snails live on land.
Some live in the sea.
And some live in fresh water.
Garden snails may eat
  our plants.
(Look up *shell*.)

snake

A snake is a reptile.
It cannot walk
But it can move
  by wriggling its backbone.
It can swim, too.

And it can climb.
A snake can move very fast.
Snakes cannot close their eyes.
They have no eyelids.

A snake can eat in one bite
    an animal much bigger
    than it is.
Some snakes eat rats and mice.
Some eat toads and frogs.
Some snakes eat insects.
Most snakes do not harm
    people.
But a few have poison fangs.
Some snakes are only
    a few inches long.
Some are many feet long.
All snakes are cold-blooded.
When the weather gets chilly,
    they curl up in a sheltered
    spot and go to sleep.
Not many snakes live in places
    with long, cold winters.
(Look up *reptile*.)

snow

Snow falls only
    when the air is cold.
Like rain, it falls from clouds.
(Look up *cloud*.)
Snow falls in flakes.
They are made up
    of tiny bits of ice
    in pretty six-sided shapes.
Snowflakes may make a thick
    blanket on the ground.
They protect plants and seeds.
So farmers like some snow
    on their fields in winter.
But too much snow
    may block country roads.
In the city snow is a bother
    to most people.
It makes walking and driving
    hard.
Snow is fun to play in.
It is fun to make snowmen
    and throw snowballs
    and play with sleds.
It is fun to go skiing, too.

S

sound

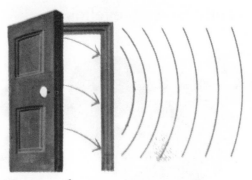

Every sound comes from
   some movement.
It must be a back-and-forth
   kind of movement.

We hear sound.
Some sounds
   make pleasing patterns.
We call them music
   or musical sounds.

Slam a door.
It shakes back and forth.
We say it vibrates.
This shaking or vibration
   moves the air around it.
The air moves in waves,
   like the ripples on a pool
   if you throw a stone in.
These waves in the air
   are called sound waves.

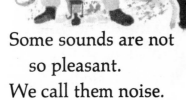

Some sounds are not
   so pleasant.
We call them noise.

When the waves reach our ears,
   our eardrums vibrate.
And we hear the sound.

Some sounds are louder
than others.
A lion's roar is louder
than a mouse's squeak.
Some sounds are higher
than others.

Sound waves travel in air
at the rate of
about 750 miles per hour.
But most sound waves
do not travel many miles.

Some planes fly faster
than sound.

A mouse's squeak is higher
than a lion's roar.
Sound waves can move
around corners.
They can move
through some walls.
They can bounce back
from other walls.

When sound waves bounce
back, we call them echoes.

Sound waves travel faster
in water or in metal
than they do in air.
Sound waves cannot travel
in empty space.
There is nothing to vibrate
there.
So there is not a sound
in space.

S

space travel

space

Space is the huge emptiness
   that stretches
   between the stars.
We often call it outer space.
Out in space
   there are other planets.
There are moons, too,
   and bits of this and that.
But most of space is emptiness.

Men want to learn
   more about space.
They want to travel
   to other planets.
(Look up *planet*.)
Airplanes travel in the air
   around the earth.
Spaceships are to go out
   where there is no air.
Space stations will be built
   out in space.
(Look up *rocket*.)

Space travelers need
    to take air and food
    and water with them.
They cannot stop
    for any on the way.
They may grow food
    in little gardens
    in the spaceship.
They have machines
    to make water and air
    pure again.
In space there is
    no up or down.
You cannot pour a glass
    of water in space.
The water will not fall down
    into the glass.

Space travelers have
    to drink water
    from "squeeze bottles."
You cannot keep your feet
    on the floor in space
    without help.
Space travelers have to be
    belted into place.
Or they will float around
    in the cabin of the ship.
There is no day or night
    in space.
Travel in space is
    a real adventure.

S

spider

spinning

A spider spins a web.
A thread of very strong,
    thin silk comes out
    from the spider's body.
This silk makes the web.
Some spider webs
    are very beautiful.

Some threads are sticky.
They catch insects
    for the spider's food.
A spider is rather like
    an insect.
But it is not one.
It has eight legs
    instead of six.
It has no feelers.
And a spider never has wings.

A spider spins silk
    from its body.
So does a silkworm.
People use tools to spin.
In spinning we start
    with thin, short threads
    or hairs of cotton
    or linen
    or wool.
They are called fibers.
We twist the fibers together.

We may use a hand spindle.
We may use a spinning wheel
    or a spinning machine
    to turn a spindle.
The turning spindle
    does the twisting.
The twisted fibers
    hold together
    in a long, strong thread.
(Look up *cloth* and *weaving*.)

stamp

A stamp is a small
  piece of paper.
It has a sticky, gummed back.
You stick a stamp on a letter.
It tells that you have paid
  for the letter
  to be sent
  through the mail.
We call it a postage stamp.
(Look up *letter*
  and *mail*.)

Each country
  has its own
  postage stamps.
Many stamps have
  tiny, pretty pictures
  on them.

Some show
  the ruler
  of the country.
Some show
  people
  of the country.
Some show
  pretty places
  in the country.
Many people collect
  postage stamps.
They keep them
  in books
  called stamp albums.
Some stamps are stuck
  on bottles
  or boxes
  or packages.
They tell
  that a tax
  has been paid.
They are called
  revenue stamps.
Some stores give
  trading stamps.
Trading stamps tell
  that we have bought things.
We save them in an album.
When the album is full,
  we can trade it for something.

S

325

star

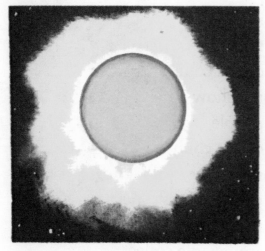

Stars shine in the sky.
The star we know best
    is our sun.
It is closest to the earth.
When the sun shines on us,
    its light is so bright
    that we cannot see
    any other star.

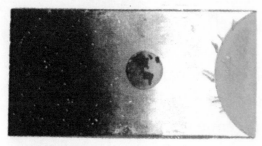

At night the sun's light
    does not shine on us.
So we can see other stars.
(Look up *day* and *sky*.)
Stars are not really star-shaped.

They are all round like the sun.
We draw them star-shaped
    because they twinkle.
Many stars are as big
    and as fiery hot
    as the sun.
Some are even bigger
    and some are even hotter.
But all stars except our sun
    are so very, very far away
    that we see them
    as just dots of light.

Some stars are red.

Some are orange.

Some are yellow.

Some are white.

Some are a little blue.

The blue stars are hottest.
White stars are next hottest.
But even red stars
    are hotter
    than we can imagine.

Scorpio

Draco

Leo

Libra

S

People in olden times
   saw pictures in the stars
   and told stories about them.
Here are some
   of the pictures they saw.
Maybe you can find
   some of them
   in the sky at night.
A few bright "stars" we see
   are not really stars.
They are planets like our earth.
(Look up *planet*.)

Big Dog

steam

When water gets boiling hot
it turns to steam.
The steam may form
a little cloud in the air.
Steam takes up more room
than the water it comes from.

If a tight cover is put
on a pan of water
and the water is boiled,
the steam will push
the cover up.
In a steam engine,
steam pushes against
part of the engine
and makes wheels turn.
It can even make a train run.
(Look up *engine*
and *locomotive*.)

steel

Steel is made of iron.
(Look up *iron*.)
Some carbon is added.
Then the mixture is heated
until it melts.
The big mills
where steel is made
have huge furnaces.

Their fires glow
night and day.

Steel is rolled
  into flat strips.
Or it is shaped
  into rails
  for railroads
  or girders
  for big buildings.

Big buildings today
  have skeletons of steel.
Where we have bones
  to make us strong
  they have girders of steel.
The girders are long beams
  put together
  with red-hot rivets
  instead of nails.
Strong tools are made
  of steel, too.

Swords for fighting men
  in days of old
  were made of steel.
That was the first use of steel.

stone

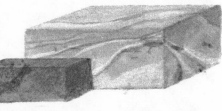

Stone is used
  in many buildings.

Before the days of steel
  all big, strong buildings
  were built of stone.
Sometimes the walls were
  many feet thick.
Pieces of stone
  have also been used

as tools,

as weapons,

as money

and
as ornaments.

S

329

storm

When a wild wind blows,
   or thunder crashes,
   or rain or snow,
   sleet or hail falls,
   we have a storm.
Storms may do a great deal
   of harm.

In a dust storm,
   the wind blows away
   dry soil
   from farmers' fields.
In a sandstorm, the wind
   blows clouds of sand
   across a desert.

The sand feels like needles
   when it hits.

In a blizzard,
   the wind
   blows the falling snow
   and piles it up in drifts.

A blizzard can block
   all the streets in a city.
It can even close schools!

A rainstorm brings rain
   and often wind, too.
Streams may flood their banks.

In a hurricane,
   the wind is very strong.
A hurricane begins
   over the sea.
It sometimes moves on
   to the land.
Wind rushes in from all sides.
But at the center
   of the hurricane
   there is no wind.
This quiet center
   is called the "eye"
   of the hurricane.
There is often hard rain
   with a hurricane, too.
In a tornado,
   the wind
   whirls in a circle.
A tornado moves very fast.
As it passes a spot
   it quickly sucks up
   roofs,
   cars,
   trees and
   furniture.

A waterspout
   is a tornado at sea.
It sucks up water
   in its whirling wind.
A thunderstorm
   is an electrical storm.
Lightning flashes
   and thunder roars.
The lightning may start fires.
There may be gusty winds
   strong enough
   to break branches
   or even uproot trees.
Rain usually falls.

An ice storm comes
with a very cold rain.
The rain turns to ice
on streets,
on trees,
on buildings.
Every stem is coated
with ice.
When the sun shines,
the whole world glitters.

Everything seems to be made
of shining glass.
But the ice is heavy.
It breaks branches.
It flattens plants.
It snaps wires.
An ice storm is beautiful
for a little while.
But the harm it does
lasts a long time.

street

A street is a road
in a city or town.
(Look up *road*.)
A business street
has shops and stores
along it.
People come to shop.
They buy things they need
and want.
There are sidewalks
for people to walk on.
At a corner
there may be a stop sign.
Or there may be a traffic light.
It tells cars and people
when to wait
and when to go.

Some streets
    are one-way streets.
All cars must go
    in the same direction
    on one-way streets.
Signs tell you
    when a street is "one-way."

Some streets are called avenues.
Some fine, wide streets
    are called boulevards.
Many streets have houses
    and lawns and trees
    along them
    instead of shops.
Streets of homes are quieter
    than business streets.

S

submarine

Sub-marine means under-sea.
A submarine is a ship
    that travels under water.
A submarine must have
    an engine to move it
    through the water.
The engine pumps in water
    to make the ship go down.
It pumps out water
    when the ship is ready
    to come up to the surface.

A submarine has a periscope.
Through it sailors on duty
    can look around
    above the surface
    from down in the water.
There are no windows
    to look out of
    in a submarine.
Sailors on a submarine
    must be men
    who do not mind
    being shut in.
They are brave sailors.

subway

A subway is a tunnel
  with a roadway
  for travel underground.
Some cities are very crowded.
The streets are full
  of cars and trucks and buses.
Often the cars and trucks
  and buses must go very slowly.
So men have dug tunnels.

Cars, trucks and buses
  run in some of the tunnels.
Trains called subway trains
  run in others.
They travel fast.
Sometimes a subway is called
  an "underground"
  or a "tube."
Subways must be well lighted.
For it is dark underground.

swimming

We have to learn
how to swim.

We swim in water.
We may swim
    in a swimming pool.
We may swim in a lake.

First we learn
    to lie down on the water.
We float.
Floating is fun.

We may swim
    at the seashore.
(Look up *lake* and *sea*.)
But we should never
    go swimming alone.

Then we learn to kick
    our legs.
We learn to pull ourselves
    ahead with our arms.
We are swimming.
What fun it is!

table

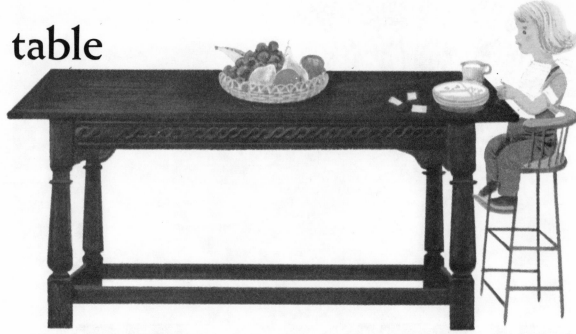

A table has a flat top
   and legs.

The table top may be wood
   or metal.

It may be glass.
It may be marble.

The table legs may be
   high enough for your knees
   to fit under the top
   as you sit on a chair.

The table legs may be so low
   that you can reach the top
   as you sit on the floor.
There are many kinds of tables.
How many kinds do you have?

tadpole

A tadpole is a baby frog
   or toad.
It lives in the water
   of a pond.
It is mostly head and tail.
At first it has no legs.
It does not look
   like a grown-up frog
   or toad at all.
It nibbles little plants
   growing in the pond.

Little by little
   a tadpole changes.
Its front part fills out.
It begins to grow legs.
First back legs appear.
Then front legs appear.
Its tail shrinks.

Before long it climbs up
   out of the water
   and breathes in air.
It is no longer a tadpole.

The little toad or frog
   eats worms and insects.
It gets bigger and bigger
   until it is full-grown.

taxi

A car you can hire
   to take you somewhere
   is called a taxi or taxicab.
Most taxicabs have a meter.
The meter measures
   how much you will pay.
In some lands
   there are not many cars.

T

A taxi may have
a motorcycle to move it.

Or it may have a bicycle.
In some places
people may hire
horse-drawn carts
to take them places.

The carts may be
two-wheeled carts
with one seat facing forward
and one back.

In a few places
a man pulls a cart for hire.

Or several men may push
and pull on hills.

In the mountains
men may carry
a sedan chair on poles.
Some cities are built
on lakes
or rivers
or canals.

They may have water taxis.
A water taxi may be
a shiny new motorboat.
It may be a gondola
pushed with a pole.
Or your water taxi
may be a shikara
paddled over the water.
It is fun to travel
in different kinds of taxis
in different lands.

telephone

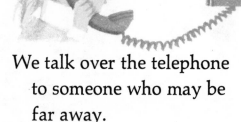

We talk over the telephone
  to someone who may be
  far away.
"Tele-" at the start of a word
  means "far away."
A telephone can bring sound
  from far away.
Electricity makes this possible.
Suppose you want to talk
  to a friend.
Then your telephone line
  is connected to his
  at the telephone office.
A current of electricity flows
  through the wires.

The sound waves of your voice
  make the electric current
  get stronger and weaker.
In your friend's phone
  the current is changed back
  into sound waves.
The sound waves strike
  your friend's ear.
And he hears you
  even though you may be miles
  and miles away from him.
Your friend can talk to you, too.
And you can hear.
(Look up *sound*.)

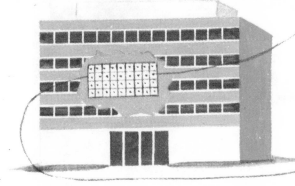

T

telescope

A telescope helps us see
things far away.
We use telescopes to look
at the moon and planets.

Men who study the heavens
through telescopes
are called astronomers.

They use big telescopes
in buildings
called observatories.

They look bigger and clearer
through a telescope.
And telescopes show us many
stars we cannot see
with our eyes alone.

television

Television lets us see
    and hear
    things from far away.
Television is radio
    with pictures.
(Look up *radio*.)
Most television starts
    in a broadcasting studio.
Cameras take the pictures.
Microphones
    pick up the sounds.

Then both sounds and pictures
    are turned into waves
    that travel through the air.
The aerial at your house
    picks up some of these waves.

In your television set
    some waves are changed
    back into sound.
Some are changed
    to make the pictures you see
    on your television screen.
And the changes from waves
    to sounds and pictures
    take less time
    than the tick of a clock.

T

343

theater

A theater is a place
where a story
is acted out on a stage.
We usually call
this kind of story a play.
If it has a lot of music
it may be an opera
or an operetta.
(Look up *opera*.)
A theater may be out of doors.
The seats may be on a hillside.

The stage may be down below.
A theater may be very small.
The actors may be dolls.

This is a puppet theater.
(Look up *puppet*.)
A theater may be in a school.
One of the actors may be you!

thermometer

A thermometer tells us
how warm or how cold
something is—
a room,
an oven,
the out-of-doors.
A thermometer
outside the window
tells us how warm
or cold the air outside is.
It has a tube
with colored liquid in it.
The liquid gets bigger
as it gets warm.
It takes more room.
So it goes higher up the tube.
The number where it stops
shows the temperature.

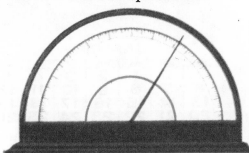

If the day grows colder,
the liquid shrinks.
It takes less room.
The liquid goes down
in the tube.
We say the temperature
is lower.
If you do not feel well,
your mother
may take your temperature.
She puts a thermometer
in your mouth.

Then she sees how far
up the tube the liquid goes.
If your temperature is too high,
you have a fever.
There are other kinds
of thermometers, too.
In some, coils of wire
tighten when they warm up
and loosen when they cool.
In some thermometers
a pen draws a line
to show the temperature.

T

tiger

A tiger is a very big animal.
It is strong and brave and wild.
It has stripes in its fur.
They help it to hide
    in the shadows
    of grass and trees.
Tigers eat meat.
They hunt animals to eat.
Some tigers are kept in zoos
    and circuses.
You may see one there.
(Look up *cat*.)

time

Time passes.
We count or measure
    the time in a day
    in hours and minutes
    and seconds.
Sixty seconds make one minute.
(A second is as short
    as the tick of a clock.)
Sixty minutes make one hour.
Twenty-four hours make
    one day-and-night.
(Look up *day and night*.)
We tell the time of day or night
    by clocks and watches.
(Look up *clock* for more
    about clocks and watches.)
We count or measure
    days as they pass
    in weeks and months
    and years.

Calendar

JANUARY

SUN.	MON.	TUE.	WED.	THU.	FRI.	SAT.
		1	2	3	4	5
6	7	8	9	10	11	12
13	14	15	16	17	18	19
20	21	22	23	24	25	26
27	28	29	30	31		

A week is seven days.
A month is about the time
   from one full, round moon
   to the next full, round moon.
Or from one sliver moon
   to the next sliver moon.
It is named for the moon—
   a mo(o)nth.
(Look up *moon*.)
Twelve months make one year.
Men label the time of year
   by months and seasons.
From one hot season
   to the next hot season
   is a year.

From one cold season
   to the next cold season
   is a year.
(Look up *seasons*
   and *calendar*.)
From the beginning of one month
   to the next time
   that month comes around
   is a year.
From one birthday
   to the next birthday
   is a year.
You measure your age in years.
Your age changes
   as time goes by.

tool

We hold tools in our hands.
Tools help us get things done.
They help us
    do our work better
    than we could do it
    without them.

We cut with a knife
    or scissors
    or a saw.

We could not do this work well
    without a tool.
We dig with a shovel
    or a trowel
    or a pick.

We pound nails with a hammer.

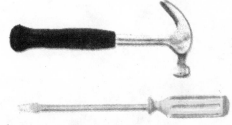

We turn things
    with a screwdriver
    or pliers
    or a wrench.

We smooth things
    with a file
    or a plane.

We clean the house
    with mops
    and brooms
    and brushes.

We keep neat
   with hairbrushes
   and toothbrushes
   and combs.

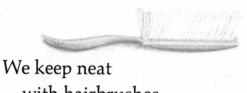

We eat with knives
   and spoons
   and forks.

We cook with spoons
   and beaters
   and cutters.

At school we use
   pencils
   and rulers
   and erasers.

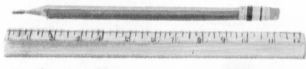

In the garden we use
   hoes and rakes.

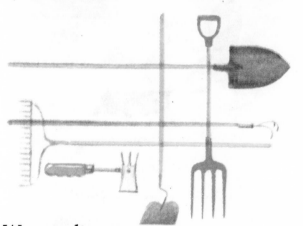

We use many tools
   in fixing foods.

We use clippers
   and garden shears.
We use some tools every day.
They help us with our work.

toy

We play with toys.
We make believe
   with dolls and doll houses,

with toy trains

and block buildings
and toy animals.
(Look up *doll* and *puppet*.)

We play at being grown-up
   with toy cooking sets,

toy stoves,
toy garden tools,

toy printing presses,
and toy doctor sets.
We learn a lot with some toys.
We have toys to pull
   and toys to fly.
We have toys to float
   and toys to ride.
We have toys to make music,
   or just noise!
We have toys for games
   and exercise.
All children like toys.

traffic

Traffic is the movement
of all the people and cars
and trucks and buses
on the streets and roads.
There is so much traffic
that we need traffic rules.
Traffic rules tell drivers
and walkers what to do.
Traffic policemen watch
to see that people
obey the rules.
And traffic policemen
help to keep us safe.

Traffic lights tell people
when to stop and go.
There are traffic signs
and road signs
to tell us many things.
(Look up *highway* and *road*.)

travel and transportation

We travel when we go
   from place to place.
We may travel by automobile.
We may have a trailer, too.
We may travel by bus.
We may travel by airplane,
   or by ship,

or by train.
(Look up *aircraft* and
   automobile.)

(Also look up *bus*.

Read about trains
   under *railroad*.

Look up *ship*
   to find out more about travel.)
They are all
   means of transportation.
They take people
   from place to place.
But trucks and trains
   and ships and planes
   do more.
They carry food and
   many supplies we need.

Transportation—
   moving people and goods—
   is a very important business.

tree

Trees are the biggest plants.
Like most plants,
    trees have roots underground.
They have stems above ground.
They have green leaves.
Most of them have flowers.
From the flowers come seeds.

From the seeds
    new trees can grow.

The seeds of some trees
    are in fruits or nuts.
Many of these are good to eat.
(Look up *flower, fruit, nut,
    plant* and *seed*.)

The seeds of some trees
    are in cones.
These trees are called conifers.
Most of the conifers
    have long, narrow leaves
    called needles.
Many trees live
    for a hundred years or more.
Some are thousands of years old.
A tree's roots keep growing
    underground.

T

353

The main stem of a tree
  we call the trunk.
It keeps growing.
In most trees
  a layer of new wood
  is added to the trunk
  every year.
It is just under the bark.
And at the tip
  of every branch
  and small twig
  there is a little new growth
  every year.
The tree's crown
  of branches and twigs
  and leaves
  grows wider and higher
  every year.
Trees are very useful plants.
Their roots hold rain water
  in the soil.
Their leaves give us cool shade.
Their branches hold the nests
  of many birds.
Their juices give us rubber
  and maple syrup
  and other things.

Their fruits and nuts
  give us food.
Their trunks give us wood
  for many uses.
And trees are beautiful.
(Look up *forest, lumbering,*
  rubber and *wood* to find out
  more about trees.)

typewriter

With a typewriter
  you can learn to write fast.
And the letters look like letters
  in a book.
A typewriter has keys
  for all the letters
  of the alphabet.
Each of these keys is fastened
  to a metal letter.
When you hit a key,
  its metal letter
  types the letter
  by pressing ink
  onto a sheet of paper.

umbrella

An umbrella protects us
from rain or too much sun.

Some sun umbrellas
are called parasols.
Some are beach umbrellas.
An umbrella folds up.
When you open it,
stiff spokes spread out.
They stretch the cover smooth.
(Look up *rain clothes*.)

umiak

A umiak is a boat
covered with skins.
Eskimos use umiaks
to carry several people.
A kayak is an Eskimo skin boat
to hold just one man.
(Look up *Eskimo*.)

unicorn

A unicorn
is a make-believe
animal.
It has a single horn
on its forehead.
Stories of days of old
tell of knights
searching for unicorns.
The stories say
that it was always
very difficult to catch one.

valentine valley

We send valentines
  on St. Valentine's Day.
It is February 14th.
A valentine tells someone
  that we like them.
It may have hearts
  and flowers
  and birds on it.
It may have a verse.

The very nicest valentines
  are those we make ourselves
  or those other people
  make for us.

A valley is the low land
  between hills or mountains.
A stream or river
  may run down it.
There may be a village
  and farms in the valley.
In a big river valley
  there may be cities.
Mountains are often
  cold and rocky.
Most valleys are pleasanter,
  greener places.

vegetable

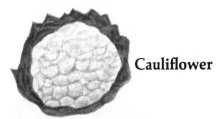
Cauliflower

We eat vegetables.
We eat some every day.

Carrots

Yams   **Turnip**

All vegetables come from plants.
Some are roots of plants.

Cauliflower's name tells
   what it is.

Peas

Some vegetables are seeds.
Some are the part of a plant
   that holds the seeds.
Tomatoes and squashes are.
Onions are bulbs.

vicuña

Asparagus

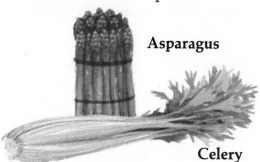

Celery

Some are stems of plants.
Stalks of celery
   are leaf stalks.

Cabbage   **Lettuce**

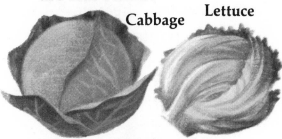

Many vegetables are leaves.

Brussel Sprouts

The vicuña is shy.
It lives
   in high mountains.
Its wool is very, very soft.
Men would like
   to raise vicuñas in herds
   for their wool.
But vicuñas will not be tamed.
They must be wild and free.

V

vine

A vine is a plant
   with a weak stem.
It cannot stand alone.
It may creep
   on the ground.
Or it may climb
   on a wall
   or a tree
   or a fence
   or a trellis made for it.

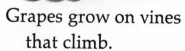

Grapes grow on vines
   that climb.
Pumpkins and squash
   and cucumbers grow
   on vines that creep.
So do watermelons.

volcano

A volcano is a kind
   of mountain.
Hot melted rock
   from deep inside the earth
   comes up
   through a hole.
The hot melted rock
   runs over the ground.
It is called lava.
The lava cools and hardens.
Cinders and ashes may blow
   up through the hole, too.
The lava and cinders and ashes
   pile up into a mountain.
In the top of the mountain
   there is a crater.
From the crater, the hole
   leads deep into the earth
   where the rock
   is fire-hot.

wall

Walls make the sides
  of rooms and houses.
They may be built of mud,
  wood, brick, metal, stone
  or even glass.
There may be windows or doors
  in them.
A room may have wallpaper
  on its walls.
Wallpaper is pasted on
  in strips.
It comes in pretty colors
  and patterns.

Solid fences around fields
  and grounds
  are sometimes called walls.

Wide walls of brick or stone
  were built around cities
  in days of old.

People could walk on top
  of these wide city walls.
The walls kept out enemies.
They had strong gates
  to let people in or out.

walnut

Walnuts grow on walnut trees.
They are seeds of the trees.
Walnuts are good to eat.
The wood of walnut trees
  makes good furniture.
It makes beautiful bowls, too.

walrus

The walrus lives in icy seas.
It is related to the seal.
It uses its long tusks
   to dig clams to eat.

wampum

In early America
   some Indians
   used wampum for money.
Wampum was made of beads
   carved from shells.
The beads were strung together.
Sometimes they were made
   into belts or necklaces.
(Look up *money*.)

washing

Every day
   we wash
   ourselves
   to get clean.
We put warm water
   into a washbowl or tub.
We use soap
   and a washcloth.
Every week we wash our hair.
Our clothes are washed
   in a washing machine.
(Look up *laundry*.)

Your father may wash the car
   with a hose
   and a sponge.
He may have it washed
   with spray
   at an auto laundry.
Streets are washed sometimes
   with spray from a truck.

wasp

A wasp
   is a flying insect.
Like bees, wasps can sting.
But they are slimmer than bees.
Some wasps live alone.
Some live with others.
Some wasps make nests
   of a sort of paper.
They make the paper
   themselves.
They chew up wood for it.
Some wasps make their nests
   of mud.

water

Water is a liquid.
It makes things wet.
Water has no shape.
It takes the shape
   of whatever it is in.
If it is pure,
   water has no color.
You can see through it.
It has no smell.
It has no taste.

When it becomes very cold,
   water freezes into ice.
(Look up *ice*.)

When it becomes boiling hot,
   it turns into steam.
(Look up *steam*.)

watch

A watch tells time.
It is smaller than a clock.
(Look up *clock*.)

Water has many uses.
We need water
   in our kitchens
   and our bathrooms.
We need water for cooking
   and for washing.
We need water to drink.

The water we use
   may come from snow melting
   in the mountains.
It may come from a river.
It may come from a lake.

It may come from a well.

Most of the earth's water
   is in the sea.
But sea water is too salty
   to drink.

Men can take out the salt,
   but doing this costs too much
   for *most* cities to use
   water from the sea.
A city may have to get its water
   from far away.

Under every city
   there are big pipes
   called water mains.
Smaller pipes
   take the water
   into our houses
   and other buildings.
When we turn a faucet,
   out it comes, ready to use.

365

Plants need water.
Most of them have roots
    that soak up water
    from the ground.

In some places there is not
    enough rain for crops.
There men often dig ditches
    to bring water
    from rivers, lakes or wells
    to the fields.
Watering fields in this way
    is called irrigation.
Animals need water, too.

Water can be made to work
    for us.
A stream of water
    may turn a water wheel.

The turning wheel
    may run a machine.
(Look up *machine*.)

A water wheel
    may turn a machine
    that grinds grain into flour.
A water wheel
    may help make electricity.

wave

You are sure to have seen
   waves in water.
Gentle breezes
   stir up little waves
   called ripples.
Strong winds
   blow up giant waves
   that often have whitecaps.
Not all waves
   are in water.
Sound and light
   move in waves, too.
Radio waves bring radio
   and television
   to us.
We cannot see
   the waves
   of sound
   and light.
We cannot see
   radio waves.
But we know about them.
How important they are!

weather

The weather may be rainy
   or snowy.
It may be sunny.
It may be cloudy and gray.
It may be hot or cold.
Winds may blow.
There may be a storm.
Weather is important
   to our work and play.

The weatherman tries
   to tell us what weather
   is coming.
Then we can prepare for it.
If he says it will rain,
   we carry raincoats
   or umbrellas.
If he says it will freeze,
   gardeners can cover
   their young plants.

weaving

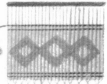

We weave by lacing
   threads or strips
   over and under
   other threads or strips.

Baskets are woven with reeds
   and grasses.
Cloth is woven with threads.
It is woven on a frame
   called a loom.

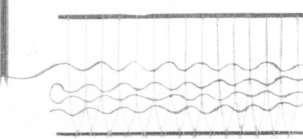

One set of threads
   is strung up on the loom.
This set is called the warp.
Another set is woven
   in and out across the warp.
These threads are called
   the weft.

Some cloth is woven by hand.

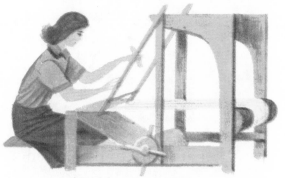

But today most cloth
   is woven on big machines
   called power looms.

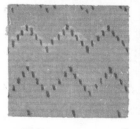 

Weaving is done in all sorts
   of patterns.
By using threads
   of different colors
     we can even weave pictures.
A tapestry is a woven picture.

weight

We weigh things on scales
  to find out
    how heavy they are.
  (Look up *scales*.)

We count weight in tons
  and pounds and ounces.
It takes 16 ounces
  to make 1 pound,
  and 2000 pounds
  to make 1 ton.
We buy coal by the ton.
We buy sugar and meat,
  butter and flour
  by the pound.
We buy dried beef and raisins,
  pepper and paprika
  by the ounce.

well

A well is a hole
  dug in the ground.
A water well is dug down
  to where underground water
  trickles through rocks or soil.
An oil well is dug deep down
  to a pool of oil
  in the rock
  deep underground.

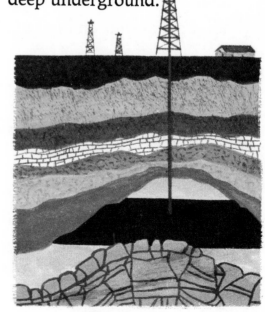

whale

There are other whales, too.
Dolphins and porpoises
are small whales.

Sperm whales are very big.
But blue whales
  are even bigger.
They are the biggest animals
  on land or sea.
A blue whale makes
  an elephant look small.
Even a blue whale baby, or calf,
  is bigger than an elephant.
The blue whale is bigger
  than the biggest dinosaur
  that ever lived.

(Look up *dinosaur* and *narwhal*.)

Whales live in the sea.
But they are not fish.
They are mammals.

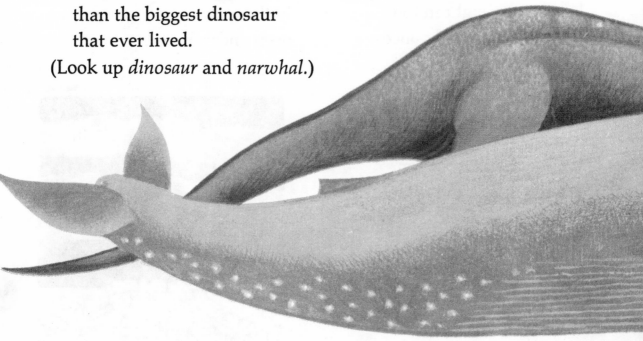

They have some hair.
They breathe in air
   and spout it out
   through blowholes
   in the top of their heads.
They give birth to babies
   instead of laying eggs.
And they feed
   their babies milk.

wheat

We make flour from wheat.
We make bread from flour.
We all eat bread.
So wheat is very important.
Wheat is a grass.
It is grown in big fields.
When the seeds, or grains,
   are ripe, it is cut.
The seeds are knocked
   off the stems.
This step is called threshing.
The grain
   is taken to a mill.
It may be ground into flour.
It may be made
   into breakfast food.
(Look up *flour*.)

wheel

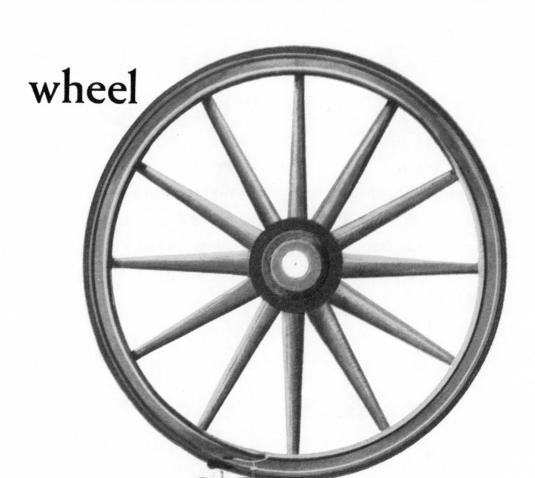

A wheel is round.
A wheel turns.
Turning wheels
    move our bicycles and cars,
    our trains and buses.

Turning wheels
    run most of our machines.
Many wheels have a rim
    around the outside
    and spokes going
    into the middle.

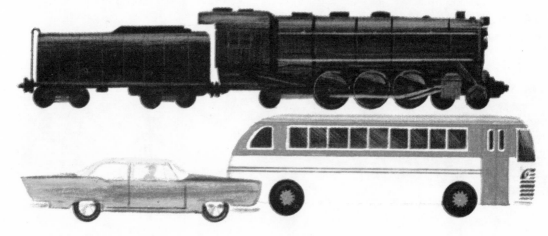

Some wheels have teeth
   in their edges.
The teeth fit
   into teeth on other wheels.
As one wheel turns,
   it turns the others.
Such wheels are called gears.

An airplane has landing wheels.
A Ferris wheel
   is a very big wheel.
A merry-go-round
   is a big wheel, too.
It is lying on its side.

(Look up *circle*.)

W

wind

Wind is moving air.
It may do work
   pushing boats, flying kites
   and turning mills.
It may blow up a storm.
(Look up *air*,
   sailboat and
   storm.)

windmill

A windmill has a wheel
   that is turned by the wind.
As the wheel turns,
   it may work a pump
   to raise water from a well.
Or it may work a mill
   to grind corn or wheat.

wind-bell

A wind-bell tinkles
   when a soft wind blows.
It makes a pleasing sound.
Wind-bells may be made
   of glass or wood or metal.
(Look up *bells*.)

wombat

Wombats look like small bears.
They are cousins
    of the koalas,
        which look like bears, too.
And they are cousins
    of the kangaroos.
A mother wombat
    carries her baby in a pouch.
Wombats dig tunnels.
They live underground.
They come out at night
    to eat grass
    and roots and bark.

wood

A wood is a grove of trees.
It is not as big as a forest.
A small wood on a farm
    may be called a woodlot.
It may be called a woodland.
The hard part of a tree
    is called wood, too.
(Look up *lumbering*
    and *tree*.)

Woodcutters cut down trees
    to get wood.
Wood cut for heating a house
    is kept in a woodpile.

W

woodchuck

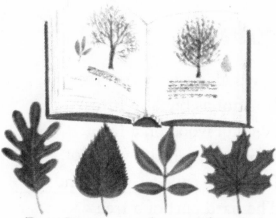

Boy Scouts study woodcraft.

They learn
  about the trees
  and other plants
  and the birds
  and other animals
  in the woods.
They learn how
  to find their way
  in the woods
  and how to camp there.

Woodchucks dig burrows
  underground.
They sleep in them
  all winter.
We say they hibernate.
Woodchucks are also called
  groundhogs.
There is a story about them.
It says that the groundhog
  comes to the mouth
  of his burrow
  on February 2nd.
If he sees his shadow,
  he knows winter will last
  six more weeks
  and he goes back to sleep.
This is just a story.
But we call February 2nd
  Groundhog Day.
We look to see if the sun
  is shining enough
  for the groundhog
  to see his shadow.

woodpecker   wool

Wool is the thick hair of sheep.
Men cut it off with shears.

Woodpeckers are birds
  that peck holes into wood.
They have sharp beaks.
Rat-a-tat-tat they go.
They eat insects
  they find in the wood.
They peck holes for nests, too.

The wool is combed
  to straighten it.
We say it is carded.
Then the wool is twisted
  into yarn.
Twisting into yarn
  is called spinning.
The yarn is woven into cloth.
Wool cloth is soft and warm.
(Look up *cloth, spinning*
  and *weaving.*)

377

worm

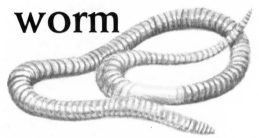

The earthworm is the worm
   we know best.
An earthworm wriggles.
Most worms do.
They have no legs.
They have to wriggle to move.
But some worms swim.
This sea mouse does.

Earthworms live in the ground.
They burrow in it
   by eating their way
   through the soil.
They make the soil richer.
Their burrows help
   to let air and water
   get into the soil.

writing

Run, Tom, run.

We write words
   by putting letters together.
We write stories
   by putting words together.
We learn to write in school.
Writing is not good
   unless people can read it.
Our writing gives people
   a message from us.
We write by hand
   with a pencil or pen,
   with crayons or chalk.
The letters we write
   look different from letters
   printed in a book.
(Look up *letter* and *alphabet*.)
Long ago people drew pictures
   instead of writing words.
We call their writing
   picture writing.

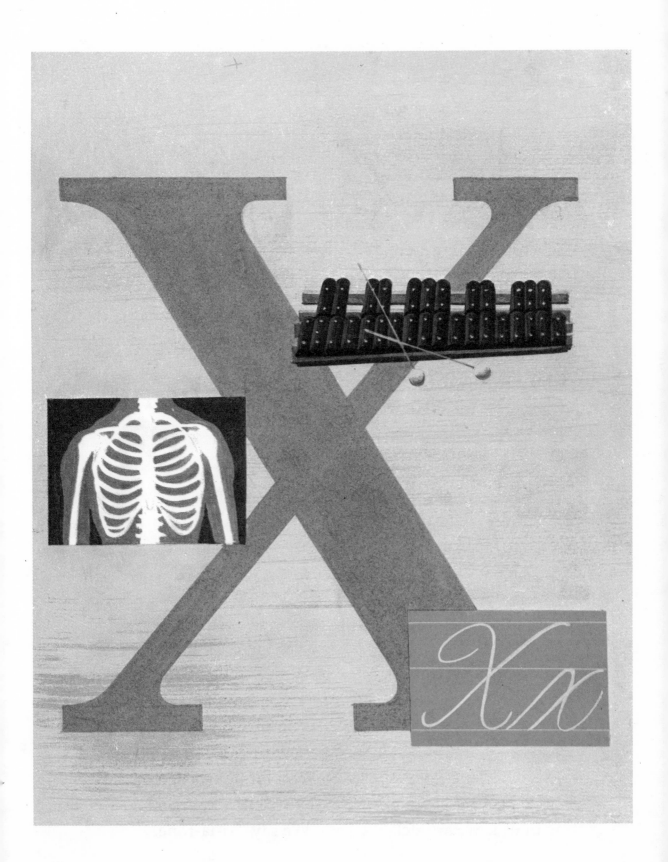

xebec

A xebec is a sailing ship.
(Look up *sailboat*.)
A xebec has three masts.
Pirates used to like to sail them.
Pirates were robbers of the seas.
We say the name "zee-bec."

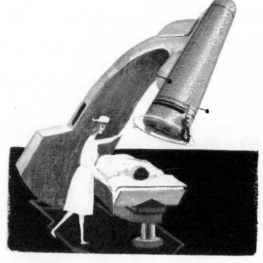

X-rays can help
   make sick people well, too.

x-ray

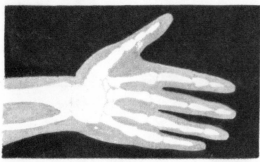

X-rays can travel through us.
They can make pictures
   of our bones.
They can make pictures
   of our hearts and stomachs
   and other organs inside us.
X-rays can help doctors
   find out what is wrong
   with us if we are sick.

xylophone

With a xylophone
   you can make music.
You play a xylophone
   with wooden hammers.
You hit its wooden bars
   with the hammers.
We say "zi-la-fone."

yak

A yak is a kind of ox.
It grows very long hair.
This long hair keeps it warm
   in the cold mountains
   where it lives.
Yaks carry heavy loads.
They give milk.
Their long hair
   makes good rope and cloth.

A person may carry two buckets
   or baskets at a time
   by hanging them from a yoke.

yolk

The yolk of an egg
   is the yellow part.
When a baby chick
   is growing inside an egg,
   the yolk gives it food.

yoke

Oxen wear a wooden yoke
   across their shoulders
   when they pull an oxcart.

yo-yo

A yo-yo
   is
   a kind
   of top.
It rolls up
   and down
   a string
   instead of spinning on a point.

Y
Z

zebra

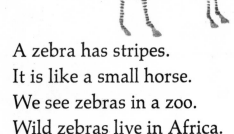

A zebra has stripes.
It is like a small horse.
We see zebras in a zoo.
Wild zebras live in Africa.

zipper

A zipper zips
    up and down.
It closes and opens jackets,
    dresses, skirts, pants
    and boots.
It has teeth that slide together
    and lock.
Sometimes a zipper sticks.

zither

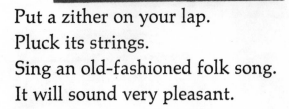

Put a zither on your lap.
Pluck its strings.
Sing an old-fashioned folk song.
It will sound very pleasant.

zoo

A zoo is a park.
Animals are kept there.
We go to see them.
We learn about animals
    of many lands.
A zoo's full name
    is zoological garden.